CLAIRE DUFFY is an English teacher and Director of Debating and Public Speaking at The Scots College in Sydney. Claire has held senior positions in government and non-profit organisations. She is the author of *The Australian Schoolkids' Guide to Debating and Public Speaking*.

The Australian Students' Guide to Writing and Grammar

Claire Duffy

NEWSOUTH

A NewSouth book

Published by
NewSouth Publishing
University of New South Wales Press Ltd
University of New South Wales
Sydney NSW 2052
AUSTRALIA
newsouthpublishing.com

© Claire Duffy 2019
First published 2019

10 9 8 7 6 5 4 3 2 1

This book is copyright. Apart from any fair dealing for the purpose of private study, research, criticism or review, as permitted under the *Copyright Act*, no part of this book may be reproduced by any process without written permission. Inquiries should be addressed to the publisher.

ISBN: 9781742236001 (paperback)
 9781742244419 (ebook)
 9781742248851 (ePDF)

 A catalogue record for this book is available from the National Library of Australia

Design Josephine Pajor-Markus
Cover design Design by Committee

All reasonable efforts were taken to obtain permission to use copyright material reproduced in this book, but in some cases copyright could not be traced. The author welcomes information in this regard.

To Mum and Michael and Nell,
with love and thanks.

CONTENTS

Introduction 1

How to use this book 10

Part 1: Good grammar, great writing 13

1   Nouns 16

2   Adjectives 24

3   Verbs 33

4   Pronouns 58

5   Adverbs 75

6   Prepositions 79

7   Articles 84

8   Conjunctions 85

Part 2: Essential skills for writing well 93

1. Spelling 94
2. Vocabulary 104
3. Punctuation 108
4. Sentences 125
5. Syntax: get your words in order 140
6. Tone: reaching your audience 145
7. Paragraphs 147

Part 3: How to be a good writer 153

1. Planning 156
2. Drafting and writing 168
3. Editing and proofreading 189

Part 4: Writing for marks 199

1. Grades explained 201
2. Creative writing 205
3. Persuasive writing 221
4. Analytical writing 232

Part 5: Writing support 247

1 Words that work 248

2 Editing 255

3 Creative plots: genres explained 257

4 More advanced grammar 261

Acknowledgments 269

Index 271

INTRODUCTION

You need to read this

You can already use the English language. You do so every day, but do you ever think about the structure and arrangement of what you say and write? And why it's said and written like *that* and not some other way? Has anyone ever asked you to catch a red big ball? No. Because in English we would say 'big red ball'. Why is that?

Welcome to the wonderful world of English words. Just imagine where we'd be without them. Impossible! For a start we wouldn't be able to communicate much. Sure, it could be done (you can try using images and pictograms for the fun of it), but words, words, words … Words really do some WORK. Whether it's spoken conversation, or writing things down, or even deeply and silently talking inside your head (yes – scientists say we need words to think), words are the most amazing building blocks of a much bigger edifice (new word? look it up!). It's called LANGUAGE.

At school you have to learn grammar. You probably know about verbs and nouns, maybe even adjectives and adverbs. Many people can't go much further than that, but you might be a smart one. Perhaps you can tell the difference between a phrase and a clause, and you might even know a subject from an object (are you still with me?). Of course, you must also learn to get your spelling and punctuation right.

Lots of people find it a chore, and no wonder – how do you enjoy studying something when you're not sure why you need to know it?

That's where we are going to focus our attention. Good grammar is your secret weapon, your booster fuel, the special ingredient that will turn you into a good – maybe even a great – writer.

Selecting the best words, stringing them together so that they make sense, saying what you mean and sounding good, all at the same time, is as much an accomplishment as high diving or playing the violin. The big difference is that with language, you already know what you're doing. You just don't know that you know.

Writing better

If you learn how English is made, it stands to reason you will use it better. You know the tools available to you and use them with confidence. With an understanding of grammar, spelling and punctuation you'll write more clearly and express yourself better. You'll develop your own style. You will know how to put colour and mood

Introduction

into your writing. When you find yourself with tingles up your spine or glued to a book that you can't bear to leave, you'll appreciate what the writer did to get that effect. It will be exciting and interesting. You too can experience the sublime sensations that words can create. The possibilities are dazzling.

You will also find it much easier to learn another language. Understanding English is a great help when you need to learn about those different parts of another language. For a start you will recognise all the names and labels we apply. Terms like 'parts of speech', 'case' and 'person' are used all the time by teachers of other languages.

Basic skills (that most students don't have)

You can't play a sport, or an instrument, unless you have a set of basic skills. That's why you go to training or have to practise. No one is born being able to shoot goals or thrill an audience with their performance. You need to learn how to do it. Sure, some people have more talent than others, but all people need to learn what to do. Being confident that you can use good grammar, spelling and punctuation is at best going to open new doors for you; at worst, it will save you from embarrassing yourself by making silly mistakes.

When I was a child, back in the Pleistocene era, we were taught grammar in primary school, to a level that most university students don't attain these days. For many students, this was a painful process of putting labels on words and taking sentences apart. It got boring pretty quickly. A few dweebs like me loved it, but on the whole it just put kids off. The reason is that they had never been told why it mattered. But it does matter, it really does.

Also – if you're a student, it is going to improve your marks.

In Australia we test the English language skills of all students in years 3, 5, 7 and 9. These tests mean we have an idea of how well the whole school population is doing. Interestingly, a pattern seems to be emerging in which students who do really well in English at a young age are not always so far ahead of the pack by the time they're in year 9. Some researchers think we don't ask enough of our young people, that students master the basics in primary school but they are not challenged enough as they grow older. They plateau in high school and don't reach their full potential as writers, because we teachers don't demand enough of them.

I think that's a bit sad. It's as if you ate a raw potato and a stick of celery and washed it down with a glass of water without knowing that boiling it all up together would give you a delicious cup of soup. Maybe you're happy that way. But let's say you do realise there's more glamorous and interesting food out there, but you just don't know how to go about preparing it.

Introduction

Help is at hand

Let's pretend that somehow you wind up in the kitchen of a 5-star restaurant. It's nothing like your kitchen at home. It's amazing, maybe confusing, full of intriguing implements: knives with strange blades, bowls and dishes in weird shapes, grinders and hammers and tweezers and tongs, and hand-held gizmos whose reason for existing is a mystery. And what's with the cooks' white jackets and the hairnets? And how come they don't seem to use each other's names?

With help you can learn what all those implements are, but more importantly you can learn how to use them. You'll need to learn about ingredients, and how they work together, and that there are different ways of preparing them, and that it's important to choose the right tools for the meal you want to make. You will practise doing all this (because cooking is a practical skill). Pretty soon you'll be concocting dishes that will have you smacking your lips. Move over *MasterChef*!

This book is not a catalogue, or a complete description of every language device there is. You can easily find all that online.

I want you to think of this book as being like that 5-star kitchen. You've probably got the English basics under control already, but there's just so much more you can do if you understand the elements, how they work together and what effects you can create with them.

The study of English. Must I?

About 527 million people speak English. That makes it only the third most-spoken language in the world. Chinese is the leader, with a whopping 1.4 billion speakers. Hindi-Urdu is runner up, with 588 million speakers. So English sounds like it's a mere bronze medallist. But wait, listen to this. English is the MOST STUDIED LANGUAGE in the world, with a staggering 1.9 billion people who want to learn it. And that gargantuan group has just gained one more member. You!

Yet, despite the enthusiasm of nearly two billion other people, when I tell year 7 that we're studying English grammar once a week I don't always get a positive reaction. This is a pity. Because if I told them we were going to take something – maybe a bike – apart, and learn about its parts so that we could reassemble it and make it work better, I think I would get a positive reaction. What they don't see is that, like messing about in the bike workshop, learning grammar is really fun.

Two main ideas (both of them wrong) seem to put people off.

Wrong Idea 1: It's about rules

Teachers, parents and professors are fond of talking about the rules of grammar. Well, just between ourselves, THERE ARE NO RULES. Computer coding

Introduction

needs rules. If you break the rules and use the wrong symbol the coding just won't work. But language isn't like that.

Without saying it, we silently agree that there are grammar *conventions*, some basic systems we all understand and use and habits that we all follow. But grammar is not like a sport, or the rules of the road. No governing body ever got together and said, 'All sentences must begin with a capital letter. You must also add "s" to many nouns – not all of them – to show there's more than one thing.' That did not happen.

The so called 'rules' of English grammar (and spelling, pronunciation and punctuation for that matter) just grew up all by themselves. It's an amazingly interesting story (which is revealed in bite-sized bits throughout this book) that happened over a very long time, and during that time there have been lots of changes. In fact, it's still happening and you can spot the changes going on all around you.

Words are like people. They have a history. They have relatives and family backgrounds. Many modern English words come from Ancient Greece or Rome or France in the Middle Ages, or an older version of English. The Vikings gave us quite a few, and so did early Germans. That's why when you look at modern German you recognise words like *Kaffee, Mann, Doktor, Eis, Maus*.

- Words can be made up in one place and move to new places when their speakers go travelling. *Gourmet, filet, café, delicatessen, kindergarten, plaza, siesta, karaoke, ninja, moped* and *paparazzi* were all non-English words to start with.
- New things are invented and we need new words to name and use them (can you think of any recent examples?).
- Words meet and mix with other words, where they merge and blend, for example, *Cyberloafing, labradoodle, biopic*.
- New words come up, old useless words die out, and many words shift their meaning.

Just as we no longer dress the way our ancestors did, we're also not speaking and writing the way they did, because language is a living thing. It changes to meet our needs and to fit with who and where we are.

Here are some words that were used in Shakespeare's time to mean something quite unlike what they mean today:

Nice used to mean 'foolish' or 'silly'.
Awful meant 'awe-inspiring' (you might say *awesome*).
Physical meant 'medicinal' or 'therapeutic'.
And – best of all – *excrement* was once just 'an outgrowth of hair'.

Introduction

If you could time-travel and tell your great grandmother that you were going to the apple store to see a genius, she would be puzzled, but she would expect you to come back having bought some fruit after chatting to a brilliantly intelligent person.

Speakers and writers are always inventing new ways to say what they mean, and the language just grows and changes to let them do it. Rules are not needed. So long as we can be understood, all is well.

Wrong Idea 2: It's all about labelling

There's a bit of truth here. One of the reasons people are put off by grammar is they've got the idea they need to attach a lot of names to things. They need to know a clause from a phrase, or tell a common noun from a proper one. That's true, but the naming and labelling are not the real point. You need these labels only so that you can see how the language is put together, understand how certain effects are created and in turn use them yourself.

Imagine you're back in that kitchen, with a potato whose skin needs to come off. You could choose to do it with a small knife or a swivel-bladed peeler – and there are at least two different models of those available. Which tool will do the job better? I have no idea ... but you will make the right choice if you understand what you want to do with the potato after it's been peeled.

Choose the implement that suits your hand best, and the one that will give you the skinless potato you need for making your meal.

It's the same with grammar. If you understand how the language is put together and what effects certain devices produce, you'll be able to use it better.

HOW TO USE THIS BOOK

There are five parts to this book. The first three are the ones that really matter.

It's not a book you begin at the beginning and read all the way through to the end. Dip into it for the help you need when you need it. It's also not a book that tells you every intricate and obscure detail. I want you to love language, and to be able to use it well. I've covered what you need in order to do that – no more.

We start with the essentials, and work our way up to the advanced skills needed for writing in a way that wins marks. At the back of the book there's an optional section on advanced grammar, for those who feel they've managed the lower slopes and would now like to climb Mount Everest. You don't need to go there, but you might want to take a peek. I've also given you some lists of words to help you when you go dry and can't think what to write.

Throughout the book, **Nerd's Corner** ( ) provides inside information about English. There are also

Introduction

Warnings! (😈) and **Wise Advice** (🦉) that you should follow.

Part 1 is about how good grammar makes you a great writer. We look at **parts of speech**. These are the labels we use to describe the function a word (or group of words) performs: *nouns*, *verbs*, *adjectives*, *adverbs* and so on. You'll find out how to put them to work for you, and where you might go wrong. To continue the kitchen analogy, it's a tour of the tools, how they work and how to handle them so you don't get hurt.

Part 2 takes you through the **essential skills of writing well**: spelling, vocabulary, punctuation, sentences and paragraphs. These are important for all types of writing. At cooking school, this would be where you learn basic techniques like frying, baking and steaming; and how to make the frequently used sauces and stocks that are important for other dishes.

Part 3 looks at **how to be a good writer**. It provides 'recipes' for you to follow so that you can use the essay formats you need most often in school and at university.

Part 4 is about **writing for marks**. It contains templates and looks closely at the three major forms of writing a student has to learn to be able to do: creative, persuasive and analytical.

Part 5 offers **support for writers**, with 'cheat sheets', helpful terms and vocabulary, as well as more advanced grammatical information for those with an inner geek that needs feeding.

{PART 1}

GOOD GRAMMAR, GREAT WRITING

Grammar is just a totally informal agreement among English speakers that certain language structures and conventions are 'OK to go' at this moment, and in this place, for these particular users. (This is called 'usage' and it's an important concept. More about it later.)

We don't make this agreement consciously, but you can see it in what we do and say to each other. To use good grammar means to be competent at using English the way it's used right now, and to appreciate what is acceptable at this place and time.

In case you think that when I say 'there are no rules' I mean 'do what you want', I'm afraid you are mistaken. This system we all informally agree on is very powerful and can be rigid. If you use it well you will be respected. If you don't, the opposite will happen. It's important to understand this.

Would you walk around with your fly undone? I doubt it. If you are happy to use poor grammar, spelling and punctuation, it's like being out in the street with your fly undone. I'm guessing that if you're reading this you would not be happy to do that, so let's get started.

PARTS OF SPEECH

Part of speech is the term we use to describe the grammatical function of a word. The most common ones are noun, verb, adjective, adverb, conjunction, article and preposition.

I need to warn you right up front that parts of speech do not always stay in the same role. They are shape shifters. The same words can be found performing several different grammatical functions, depending on context, or the situation they're in.

1
NOUNS

You need nouns to name things. Easy. Nouns are the most common part of speech in English, for that simple reason.

People who study language and sort words into groups have come up with five different types of nouns. The main reason that classification is useful is because we treat some types of nouns differently from others. (As we're only at the beginning, you'll have to wait and see how this unfolds.)

The five types of nouns

1   **Common** nouns are basic names for things: feet, legs, knees, pants, shirt, neck, head, hat, brain, table, fridge, house, cat, gum. Look around, there are plenty for you to pick.
2   **Proper** nouns are specific: they name a single thing, and for doing that they are awarded a capital letter. Australia, Gerald, Government, Westmead

Hospital, New South Wales, Ms Duffy. The capital letter matters. If you can't be bothered to use one, then it's 'goodbye marks' and 'hello embarrassing myself'.

3   **Collective** nouns refer to a group. A *school* of fish, an *audience*, a *flock* of sheep, a *gang* of robbers. Be careful here. A collective noun makes many things into one, a single collection, so the language around them should show this. 'A flock of sheep *is* lost on the hillside', not '*are* lost on the hillside'. It's one whole flock that IS lost, not the many sheep that ARE within it. 'The gang of robbers *was* arrested.' (There was only one gang.) 'The audience *is* on its feet', not '*are* on their feet'. (There is only one audience.)

At least, that's what some people will tell you. Others will say that it's OK to use the plural because we are talking about multiple things. 'That flock of sheep *are* lost', and 'the gang of robbers *were* arrested'. Listen to the people around you and see what they do in this case. It's probably OK to follow along. The audience for this book is going to have to decide for itself / themselves.

4   **Abstract** nouns name things that you can't see or touch, or find anywhere in the real world. These are intangible things (from the Latin word *tangere*, meaning 'to touch'). Emotions, feelings and ideas, like love, success, sadness, interest, favour, anger

and joy are all abstract nouns. Because many children have been taught that a noun is the name for a person, place or thing, and they don't realise that 'misery' and 'hope' are things too (just things you can't touch), spotting abstract nouns can be a challenge.

5 **Compound** nouns occur when we use two words to create one noun. The words that are joined don't have to be nouns, and the new noun can either be written as two words or one. That can cause confusion. Examples are *washing machine, skipping rope, greenhouse, software, input*. There may be two words in there, but once they've been joined to refer to a single thing, they're one noun.

So that's it for the five basic types of nouns. Now for the extras.

6 **Gerunds** are so cool. They are my very favourite thing. They are a special, unique breed, with a bit of noun and a bit of verb.

Look at this sentence: 'Dancing is fun, but I also love kayaking'. Now ask yourself: are those 'ing' words nouns (because they name things?) or verbs (because they're action words?). Hard to tell, isn't it?

The answer is that they're called **gerunds**, and they're nouns. But I like to think of them as hybrids, or 'half and half'. They always end in 'ing'.

Singular and plural

Nouns have two versions or 'forms': singular (just one thing) or plural (more than one thing). I'm guessing you already know that. Mostly we make plurals in English by adding an 's', but there are so many exceptions to that statement that we could probably spend the rest of the book listing them. Here are some examples – just a taster – of some complicated irregular plurals.

man – men
mouse – mice
child – children
tooth – teeth
knife – knives
fungus – fungi
moose – moose
tomato – tomatoes
crisis – crises
criterion – criteria
sheep – sheep
radius – radii

It's a good idea to search online for yourself, as the internet is awash with lists of this type. Make sure that you know the correct plurals of the words you like to use.

Noun phrases

Sometimes, when a group of words works together as if it were a noun, we call that a noun phrase. It's hard to show these out of context, but phrases like 'The important documents' or 'Aunt Sally's cat' are both multi-word nouns. They name things. Don't get too worried about this – we don't need to work with noun phrases yet and I will explain them fully later in the book.

Nominalisation

This is nothing but a fancy way of saying 'making a noun out of something that wasn't'. It is useful, especially when you want to write in a formal way.

- The colour of the leaves *changes* as autumn comes.
- The *change* in the leaves' colour is because autumn comes.

Change was a verb the first time round, but is a noun in the rewrite.

Writing well with nouns

Because you need nouns to name things, nouns create a sense of what those things are like: how they look, sound, feel, taste and smell. You should build a healthy

> **🦉 WISE ADVICE**
>
> If you're unsure what part of speech a word is, test it by removing it and replacing it with one you are sure of. If the sentence still makes sense, you're correct. In the example under 'Gerunds' on page 18, you could try saying 'Minecraft is fun. I also like tennis', assuming you're quite sure Minecraft and tennis are both nouns. (They are.)

vocabulary so you have a good range of nouns to choose from.

1. Well-chosen, **precise nouns** convey lots of information, making your writing more interesting and varied. They create a clear, vivid scene in the mind of your reader, and they impress markers.

    For example, don't say 'bird' if you can say 'magpie' (or 'sparrow' or 'kookaburra' or whatever works in context). Maybe the garden you're describing is full of 'trees and flowers', but the reader will get one idea if they are 'oaks and daffodils', and quite another if they are 'gums and bottlebrush'.

    Your character might fall into the water, but was it the sea, a pond, a river, a puddle, a lake or the dam on the farm? Each of those words will create a completely different scene in the mind of the reader.

2. Precise nouns also let you know **when and where** something is happening: 'Across the lawn he heard the distant sound of a gramophone.'

   Gramophone tells us that we're in the early twentieth century, and are probably at a posh, grand sort of place – nice enough to have a big *lawn*.

   Imagine the difference if you wrote 'Across the paddock he heard the distant sound of a piano.'

   Now we're probably in Australia, on a farm, possibly long ago when piano playing was more common than now.

   Either one gives us much more information than simply saying 'From far off he heard music.'

3. Choosing **nouns that relate** helps you develop detail.

   Let's say you're describing the inside of a shed. What would you find there? Garden rakes, spades and shovels, a wheelbarrow? Maybe there are tins of nails, bags of fertiliser, paint brushes, rags, bottles of turps and kerosene. You don't need to list all these nouns at once, you can release them slowly, little by little throughout the story.

4. **Proper nouns (names)** provide wonderful hints at the nature of a person or a place.

   You don't need to be told that a family called Dursley who live in Privet Drive won't be very nice. (Privet is a weed in Australia, but in England, where the story is set, it's used for suburban hedges. The

Dursleys are small-minded and conventional). What about Hideaway Tom or Storm Boy? They've got something odd going on. Would you expect Cruella De Vil to come over with chicken soup next time you've got a cold? *Wuthering Heights* doesn't sound like a place to go for a holiday. (It isn't.) And as for Darth Vader – I don't need to know anything more about him. He's a bad guy.

GIVE IT A GO

Think of a place you know really well, like your bedroom, or somewhere outdoors you often like to go, and write a short description of it using precise, accurate nouns.

2
ADJECTIVES

These are the words that we add to give a noun more life, and to make it more specific and interesting. Adjectives are usually called 'describing words', and in grammar-speak we say they *modify* or *qualify* nouns, which means they make a difference to the 'boss' noun.

It's easy to find and use adjectives. Here's a list that just toppled out of my head: *big, slimy, sturdy, blue, quick, lazy, heavy, old, exhausted, sharp, transparent*. What would be good nouns to attach any of those to?

Adjectives often sit right in front of the noun they work for, as in 'the *tired* child', 'the *nutty* professor'. However, they can also be located away from their 'boss' noun. In the sentence 'the child is tired', *tired* still describes the *child*, but the linking verb *is* has pushed in and split the adjective / noun couple up. (You can read about linking verbs on pages 44 and 46.) That's OK. In fact, it's often a sign of a well-constructed, complex sentence. Exam markers LOVE it.

Adjectives don't have to be single words. Two or more words can work together to do the work of an adjective.

When they do, we call it an *adjectival phrase*. Here are some examples:

> The child is *tired of travelling*.
> The professor is *quite nutty*, and *really bad tempered*.

When you're trying to find adjectives, remember to search the whole sentence, and don't look only for single words.

Comparatives and superlatives, or 'how much is that?'

One of the great things about adjectives is that they describe *how much* of whatever it is they provide to their boss noun. It's called *degree*. It's a bit like when you adjust the heat under a saucepan – you can dial the intensity of an adjective up or down so it provides more or less of whatever-it-is. You usually do this by adding the suffix (a syllable at the end of a word) '-er' or '-est'.

Here's what I mean:

> I am old*er* than my sister, in fact I'm the old*est* in my family.

> This is weird, and getting weird*er*. It's the weird*est* thing I've ever done.

> ### 😈 *WARNING!*
>
> **Part-of-speech confusion**
>
> A word can change its function depending on the context. It's up to you to do the detective work to see which role the word is performing. It does not always have to be the same part of speech.
>
> The word *this* can be a pronoun because it stands in for a noun. But if I say 'this cat', I'm using *this* to describe the cat: it's *this* cat and not *some other* cat. *This* is now on duty as an adjective. *Each*, *every*, *either* and *neither* are also dealt with in the Pronouns section. They too can also work as adjectives; just add a noun and see.
>
> Sometimes nouns seem to be used as adjectives. How do you like your *history* teacher? Ever go to the *ball* park? Lost the *bath* plug? Do you own a *sports* car? Those words are normally nouns, but here they look like adjectives. They're not. Together with the noun that follows them, these are called compound (two-word) nouns. The way to test this is to ask yourself 'Is the plug bath?' 'Is a car sports?' As the answer is 'no', you can see they can't be adjectives.

The '-er' form is called **comparative**, because you're looking at this thing in comparison to at least one other.

If the adjective has two syllables, we usually compare by using the word *more*, rather than adding 'er' to the

Adjectives

end. And when the adjective has three syllables you definitely use *more* and don't use '-er'. For example, it would be awkward (though not wrong) to say 'I was *more lucky* than my sister', but it would be quite wrong to say 'She was *intelligenter* than I am'. I can be luck*ier*. She is *more* intelligent.

The '-est' form is called **superlative**. See how the word 'super' is in there? It comes to us from Latin and it means 'above' or 'beyond'; these days it often means 'first rate' or 'fantastic'.

A **superlative** is top of the tree. Unimprovable. It doesn't get any better. If I'm the old*est* in the family that's it, no one can beat me at that. I can also be the short*est*, smart*est* and funni*est*, but sadly not the intelligent*est*. As we just saw, intelligent can't be modified by adding a suffix, so we have to use *more* to make it comparative and *most* to make it superlative. My sister is *more intelligent* than I am (I'm just comparing the two of us), and she is the *most intelligent* in the family (best in a big group).

Some adjectives don't have any low or high-powered forms. They are absolutes. They describe a one-and-only item. We call them **non-comparable**. Think about the meaning of *unique* or *extinct*. Logically a species can't be *extincter*, and an event couldn't be *uniquer*. A *childless* person can't be more or less childless, a *wooden* boat can't be more or less wooden. Either they are or they aren't.

Because this is English, of course there are exceptions. Some adjectives have **irregular** comparatives and superlatives that don't relate obviously to each other. Common ones are:

little, less, least
much, more, most
good, better, best
bad, worse, worst

 NERD'S CORNER

The most importantest
It was once OK to add power to your superlatives by using *most* as well as the '-est' suffix (Shakespeare did it often). You could describe someone as the *most vilest* person alive. If you said that these days you'd sound uneducated.

Writing well with adjectives

Adjectives are essential for describing things. They give the details that help a reader form a clear, sharp picture in their mind. You need them to give precise descriptions, and to build atmosphere and imagery. You need them to bring a scene to life.

Precision

First let's think about **precision**. Adjectives help you tell one thing from another. Imagine a sea of school students, at Assembly perhaps. In a big group they all look much the same. Can you describe someone so that a stranger could find that person in the crowd? Not without adjectives you can't.

> My *tall*, *dark-haired* friend has *messy* hair, his *grubby* trainers are *unlaced*, and his *blue* shirt is *untucked*.

The risk with adjectives is that you can overdo it. Do you need a few adjectives for effect? If so, avoid a long list, as it tires the reader out. Just use two or three at a time. Multiple adjectives can be grouped next to the boss noun, or strung out throughout a sentence, like this:

> The little blonde child in the car is cold, tired and grumpy.

The basic connection between the boss noun and the adjectives is still there. *Little*, *blonde*, *cold*, *tired* and *grumpy* all modify the noun *child*, but separating them sounds much better than clumping them all together:

> The little, blonde, cold, tired and grumpy child is in the car.

Atmosphere and imagery

Now let's consider **atmosphere** and **imagery**. We're going to look at adjectives in action.

This is an eyewitness account of the volcano Mount Vesuvius erupting almost two thousand years ago. Fantastic descriptive adjectives make us feel as though we can see it.

> The sea seemed to roll back upon itself ... driven from its banks by the *convulsive* motion of the earth ... On the other side, a *black and dreadful* cloud, broken with *rapid, zigzag* flashes, revealed behind it *variously shaped* masses of flame ...
>
> (Pliny the Younger, *Letter to Tacitus*)

And here's someone you may recognise:

> Toto was ... a *little* black dog, with long *silky* hair and small black eyes that twinkled merrily on either side of his *funny, wee* nose.
>
> (L. Frank Baum, *The Wonderful Wizard of Oz*)

See how the adjectives help us get a sense of Toto's appearance and character? Being *little*, *silky*, *funny* and *wee* are associated with the playful pleasures of childhood. The author has chosen these adjectives for that reason. This has been written for a young audience. His purpose is to make us fond of this creature.

Adjectives

Imagine if he'd said:

> Dorothy's dog Toto was small, long-haired and black, with dark eyes and a small nose.

This is factually accurate but it wouldn't make us smile and feel warm and fuzzy about Toto.

✏️ GIVE IT A GO

Now read this description, also from *The Wonderful Wizard of Oz*. It's beautiful. You now have an assignment. Your job is to change it so it creates the opposite effect to the original. Instead of a scene of tranquillity and loveliness, you must turn it into a sinister, scary one, only by changing adjectives, which are underlined to help you.

Here's the original:

> There were <u>lovely</u> patches of greensward all about, with <u>stately</u> trees bearing <u>rich and luscious</u> fruits. Banks of <u>gorgeous</u> flowers were on every hand, and birds with <u>rare and brilliant</u> plumage sang and fluttered in the trees and bushes. A little way off was a <u>small</u> brook, rushing and sparkling along between <u>green</u> banks ...

After you've had a go, you can take a look at my spooky version of this passage on the top of page 32.

Part 1: Good grammar, great writing

MY SPOOKY VERSION

There were decayed patches of greensward all about, with leafless trees bearing old and wrinkled fruits. Banks of dying flowers were on every hand, and birds with strange and dreary plumage sang and fluttered in the trees and bushes. A little way off was a turbulent brook, rushing and sparkling along between craggy banks ...

Getting the order right – The Big Red Ball rule

You don't really need to know about this because you do it automatically, but it is fun. If a number of adjectives modify the same noun, we line them up this way: 1 size, 2 age, 3 shape, 4 colour, 5 origin, 6 material, 7 purpose.

Do you happen to have a *leather round English old red cricket big* ball anywhere round the house?

No? Perhaps you didn't fully understand my question.

How about a *big old round red English leather cricket* ball?

You do? That's amazing!

And if you have a personal opinion about that cricket ball, that comes first: It's 'a beautiful (smelly? filthy?) big old round red English leather cricket ball'.

Try and mess around with a few adjective lists of your own.

3
VERBS

Nouns and Verbs are the Adam and Eve of English. They're the founders, they get the whole thing started, and their DNA is running through everything. They exert huge influence over the Grammar family.

We have seen already how vital nouns are, but if you ask me, verbs are the king of the grammar castle. They rule. They're the motherboard, the control panel of the whole English language. You need verbs before you can talk or write about anything at all. You can't even have a sentence without a verb. That's how important verbs are.

Verbs are **doing** words, or **action** words. At least that's what you've been taught. More accurately, verbs let you know what's occurring. When you start the engine of a car, it powers up and off you go. This is what a verb does. No engine, no go. Verbs make your language move along, they cause things to happen, they give it life, bounce around, or if need be, they hold it back and settle it down.

Regular and irregular verbs

Verbs are organised in a systematic way, but only up to a point. This is English. Prepare to be confused!

Most verbs are **regular**. These verbs change to show different meanings, and they do it in a predictable way.

To create the past tense, you add 'ed' to the stem: *climb / climbed, play / played.*

When we're talking about *he*, *she* or *it* doing something we put an 's' at the end: *I love him*, but *he loves me*.

Lots and lots of English verbs operate this way. The only thing to be careful of is that if the verb ends in 'y' you might need a spelling change as you go into the past tense. *Try* and *cry* become *tried* and *cried*; *carry* turns into *carried*.

Trust me, you will not have any problems with regular verbs. If you are a native speaker they were embedded in your neural pathways long ago. If you are learning English they are pretty straightforward to practise and learn.

Here's the catch. About 200 of the most common verbs in English are **irregular**. They change to the past and move from singular to plural in unpredictable ways. You know how *swim* becomes *swam*, *drive* turns into *drove*, *ride* becomes *rode* and *go* changes to *went*. (Huh?? How did that happen?)

Importantly, the verbs we use **most often** in English are nearly all irregular. Think about these:

Say / said; make / made; take / took; know / knew;
think / thought; leave / left; bring / brought;
keep / kept.

You need these verbs (plus about 50 others) for your most basic day-to-day activities.

It's important to use irregular verbs properly. If you say something like *we have rang the bell*, or *we sung loud*, or *my jumper shrinked*, you can expect to have people look at you oddly.

What, Who and When

Without making it obvious, a verb tells you three things all at once: WHAT'S occurring, WHO is doing it, and WHEN. Let's look at them one by one.

1 What's going on?

Using verbs to say what's happening is pretty simple. The only thing you need is a good vocabulary. Choose the best verb for the job.

Having a good repertoire of verbs makes your descriptions come alive. Verbs are the masters. You shape and change the meaning of a sentence with the verb.

Let's say:

'I *go* to Mountainview School'.

NERD'S CORNER
Irregular verbs: the background story

The reason English has so many irregular verbs is because they came to us in the Dark and Early Middle Ages, when some of our ancestors spoke a Germanic language called Old English. It was brought to Britain by invading Germanic tribes. Back then (and still now, in modern German), some verbs change their stem vowel when they go into the past tense. English inherited this habit. It lives on in:

- sing / sang / sung
- swim / swam / swum
- drink / drank / drunk (to give just a few examples).

Sometimes there can also be an 'en' ending in the past tense:

- give / gave / given
- choose / chose / chosen
- bite / bit / bitten
- steal / stole / stolen
- eat / ate / eaten.

There is, of course, no reliable pattern. It's English!

One of the fun things about listening to toddlers and pre-schoolers learn to speak is that they go through a stage where they apply 'rules' incorrectly because they haven't yet absorbed the difference between the regular and irregular verbs. 'I gived' or 'me seed' are cute if you're three years old. Don't try it much later than that!

Or maybe:

'I *climb* to Mountainview School'.

New verb, new meaning!

Climb tells us that the school is way uphill. It calls attention to the way you travel there. You are talking about the trip you make there each day. This verb draws attention to *how* you get there, so your reader can imagine you with crampons, or climbing a long steep staircase, or scrambling up through the bush.

However, if you want to emphasise the school, or the fact that you are a student there – rather than how you get there – the all-purpose verb *go* in the first sentence works better. It stands back in the shadows and allows the school to shine through. It's a non-specific, general, all-purpose verb. It works in all sorts of conditions. It plays down the trip and lets us focus on you, or the school.

Let's think of another situation from daily life that could be livened up or quietened down by a well-chosen verb. How about getting ready in the morning?

Do you '*do*', *brush*, *comb*, *gel*, *scrunch*, *iron*, *blowdry* or just *ignore* your hair?

In what way do you have breakfast? Do you *eat*, *devour*, *grab*, *enjoy*, *savour* or *skip* it? (Bad idea that.)

What about the way your pet gets around? Of course, it *walks* (unless it's a fish, or maybe a snake, or a bird – well they can walk, I suppose, but it's not their first choice). Does it *run, fly, jump, gallop, swim, creep* or *climb*? Can it *lollop, lope, prance, soar, claw, slide* or *slither*?

Maybe, for fun, you could try using animal verbs for humans. The politician *slithered* into his seat. The marching band *pranced* down the street. The baby *yowled* all morning.

2 Who's doing it?

Here's something strange. The answer to this question will be a number.

In English grammar we have three 'persons' who can do things. These are called – with amazing originality – First Person, Second Person, and (how did you guess?) Third Person. *I* am the First Person (of course!), *you* are the Second Person; and *he, she* and *it* are all nobodies over there in a corner called Third Person.

Those are all 'singular' as they refer to just one, single person. They also have plural versions (*we, you* and *they*), which you can see in the table below.

Singular		Verb form	Plural		Verb form
1st person	I	walk / sit / sleep	1st person	We	walk / sit / sleep
2nd person	You		2nd person	You	
3rd person	He, she, it	walks / sits / sleeps	3rd person	They	

Here's the thing: in the **present tense**, if the doer is either *he*, *she* or *it*, you have to change the verb by adding an 's'. He / she / it goe*s*, drive*s*, ride*s*, swim*s* or climb*s*.

So, to be terrifyingly technical: third-person singular verbs in the present tense change this way.

What I'm trying to say is – it's the 's' on the end of the verb that lets you know who's doing it.

3 When?

Verbs have **tense**. This doesn't mean they are anxious and nervous. This meaning of the word 'tense' comes from an old French word *tens*, which had to do with time, or era. **Tense** is how a verb lets us know **when** something takes place.

There are three main tenses: **present**, **past** and **future**. Within each of these, there are variations, which mean we can be exact about time frames. If you are a native English speaker, tense is one of those things you do without knowing it.

However, we are going to widen your world by unpacking and explaining *how* you do it. We'll meet a few tenses you may not have heard of, and we'll learn some of the labels that grammarians use for these. It's a bit like a doctor knowing the right names for all your body bits. Being able to identify the components of the language helps you to understand the anatomy of

English. It's called **parsing**, and it means to take some language apart and figure out what all the parts are doing to make it work.

Buckle up, and let's get started.

A quick tense tour

In order to change a verb's tense you can:

1. Change the ending: *walk / walking / walked*
2. Change the stem as well as the ending if it's an irregular verb: *draw / drew / drawing / drawn; eat / ate / eating / eaten*
3. Add an extra word to make it a multi-word verb: *will* walk / *have* walked / *had* walked / *will have* walked / *am* walking / *was* walking; *can* or *might* or *could* walk.

Those extra words are 'helping' verbs. In grammar-speak they are called **auxiliary verbs**.

Verbs

Terminology time

To become a tense know-all, you'll need some definitions.

Simple	The basic form of the verb, in the present or past or future. I *sit*. I *sat*. I will *sit*.
Perfect	Used for actions which are finished. The verb has at least two words in it and one of them is *have* or *had*. I *have* sat. I *had* sat.
Continuous	For actions which are – you guessed it – continuing. It will be a two-word verb and the main verb ends in 'ing'. I was *sitting*.
Conditional	For actions which are only possibly or probably happening. It's a two-word tense and the helper words are often *may*, *might*, *could*, *should*, *would*. I *could* sit. (A complete list of conditional helper verbs is on page 42.)
Present participle	This is what we call it when the verb has an 'ing' ending, for example, *sitting*, *walking*, *swimming*.
Past participle	This is the name for a regular past tense verb with an 'ed' ending: *lived*, *painted*, *walked*. For irregular verbs, the past participle is unpredictable: *eaten*, *known*, *swum*, *brought*.

Simple tenses

When you change *I swim* to *I swam* it moves from the present to the **simple past** tense. *I will swim* adds a helping verb that sends the verb off to a **simple future**. It's an easy switch. You know how to say that *last week we went to school*. You can also let me know that *next week we will go* there. Those are all simple tenses.

Perfect tenses

If the helping verb is *have* or *had*, we call it the **perfect tense**. In this context, *perfect* means perfected, or complete. The action is, was or will be finished. For example:

> I *have waited* a long time for this. I *had hoped* for it sooner.

If you'd like the full story on perfect tenses, go to pages 264–266.

Continuous tenses

These are easy to spot because the verb has 'ing' on the end. Continuous tenses describe something that is going on, is a habit, or is something that you do often or constantly.

> I *am waiting*. I *was waiting* before you were born, and soon I *will have been waiting* for decades.

Conditional tenses

Imagine that! Unreal! Hypothetically speaking …

Sometimes you need to deal with something that hasn't happened, but it's a possibility, or likely to happen. Maybe it's something you wish for. Perhaps it depends on something else happening first – an 'if … then …' situation.

Clues that you're using the conditional are the words *may, might, would, could, should, can* and *will*. (You'll also find a few more on page 267.) They are always paired with another verb, so these are *helper* verbs: *I might go, I could go, I would go.*

> **WARNING!**
>
> ### The tense trap
> One of the worst habits of young writers is mixing tenses up. You are not a time traveller! If the actions happen in the same time period, keep the tenses the same.
>
> If you say 'I *swam* until my arms *ached*' you can't then say 'and I *dry* myself and *go* home'. That sentence has a time shift in it. It starts in the past and it ends in the present. You have to say 'and I *dried* myself and *went* home'.
>
> Look at these. Ever been guilty of writing something similar?
>
> > I <u>had</u> to think of some way to <u>fix</u> this before Dad <u>gets</u> home.
> >
> > 'Will he be alright?' <u>said</u> a woman in a voice <u>I've</u> never heard before.
> >
> > It <u>was</u> Christmas eve, my brother and I <u>can't</u> wait.
>
> If you are writing about things that do happen in different periods of time, however, of course you need multiple tenses to describe them.
>
> > The rocket *was launched* last Sunday, and *takes* three days to get to the moon, so it *will land* on Wednesday.

'To be' and the linking verbs

Some verbs are showoffs. These verbs dramatise and gush; they take the spotlight and everyone notices them. Other verbs are subtle, behind-the-scenes operators. They don't make a fuss, they're quiet, but they keep things together. These verbs are essential, and everywhere. We use them without even realising they are verbs half the time. These are the **being** and **having** verbs. They're called **linking** verbs because all they do is connect two aspects of the same thing.

The verb 'to be'

Ladeez and gentlemen! Allow me to introduce THE most essential of all English verbs. This verb is WAAAY irregular. It's a high-flying, low-diving, tumble-turning acrobat of a verb. This verb is more irregular than anything you could make up! It has relatives, family and connections and they are a crazy, mixed-up, unusual, one-of-a-kind bunch, unlike any other. It's impossible to see how they relate and what connects them. Yet, ladeez and gentlemen, this family is *vital* to English, and you use it all the time. Can you find examples of it here?

> I am tired. So are you. It is late! We were up all night.

Did you pick them? Yes indeedy! The verbs are *am*, *are*, *is* and *were*. They look completely different but they belong to one family.

And are they action words? Do they DO anything? No, they do not. In fact they're so understated that you might think I'd laid a trap. You may even be wondering where the verb in each of those sentences was.

Well, don't be alarmed; thousands have been similarly fooled. The 'action' that these verbs do is merely to tell us that something exists. I am – I exist. You are – you exist!

But what, I ask you, is the name of this verb family? You don't know? Then, what a pleasure it is to introduce you to **the verb 'to be'**.

There are eight words in this family. They are *be, am, is, are, was, were, been* and *being*. Ladeez and gentlemen, I ask you to respect and treasure these eight precious, vital words. Treat them carefully. Use them well. They are like oxygen for the English language. Without them there's no life.

William Shakespeare, that greatest of all writers in English, knew the power of the verb 'to be' when he created a character called Hamlet. Hamlet, talking to himself while in a very low state of mind, asks, 'To be, or not to be, that is the question'. Was he working on his grammar homework, ladeez and gentlemen? No, he was not! He was deciding whether to keep on living! To continue existing! That is the power of the verb 'to be'.

Helping other verbs

Not only does 'to be' mean we can say that we exist, when it comes to making sentences this family of verbs may not add much meaning by themselves, but they provide essential services to other verbs.

Their first vital function is just to connect two items in a sentence (often a noun and its adjective), and for this reason they are also called **linking verbs**. When I say 'my mind is clear', or 'the weather is cold', the word *is* links my mind or the weather to the description of it. Think of it like a maths equation:

> My mind = clear
> The weather = cold

There are a number of other verbs that can function as linking verbs, among them *appear, become, feel, grow, look, remain, seem, smell, sound, stay, taste* and *turn*.

If you're unsure whether a verb is working as a linking verb, try replacing it with part of the verb 'to be' and see if it makes sense. For example: 'School can *seem* a safe place'. We could say: 'School can *be* a safe place', so in this case *seem* is a linking verb.

Their second vital function is to provide the helping words that we met already, when we looked at two-word verbs. Many participles, like *been* and *being* can't be used by themselves. You need to add *was* (or *have / had*) as helper verbs for them to make sense.

I was being sick, when …
I have / had been sick, when …

You obviously can't say 'I being sick' or 'I been sick' unless you are happy to attract odd looks.

How verbs rule

Verbs are bossy-boots. Imagine the verb is out on the soccer field, hands on hips, whistle between teeth, yelling instructions to all the other parts of speech about where to go and what to do. Verbs are the controllers of how words are arranged in a sentence, and because of that, they shape the way meaning comes across. We are about to explore and explain how they do this.

Terminology time

You'll need four new terms to describe verbs and the parts of a sentence. If you take any sentence apart to inspect its grammatical parts (**parse** it), you will deal with some of these.

1. The **subject**.
2. The **object**.
3. If a verb has a subject it's called a **finite verb**.
4. If it has an object it's called a **transitive verb**.

Let's explain …

Subjects

If I ask you what the **subject** of a verb or a sentence is, you're going to say 'It's what it's about'. Trick question! That's a sensible answer in everyday language, but it's not correct in Grammar-land.

In the study of grammar, the term **subject** means **the thing that does the action**. To find the subject, you go to the verb and ask yourself 'Who or what is doing this?' The answer is the verb's **subject**.

> *I am the greatest.* Who is the greatest? *I* am.
> (*I* is the subject.)
>
> *She loves me.* Who loves me? *She* does.
>
> *Australia beat Sri Lanka.* Who beat Sri Lanka? *Australia* did.
>
> *Kids trapped by floodwaters.* Who was trapped by floodwaters? *Kids* were.

You get the idea?

The term for everything in the sentence, including the verb, that is not the subject, is the **predicate**.

Subject–Verb agreement

Verbs control everything, so you must agree with them. Disagree at your peril.

If your subject is singular – just one thing – the verb it goes with must also be singular: 'The table *is* set'.

If the subject is plural, of course the verb is plural as well: 'The tables *are* set'.

You'd be amazed how often students don't get this right: 'We had just moved house and there *was* cardboard *boxes* everywhere'.

Aieee! Not right! Never was. Never will be.

Finite and non-finite verbs

The word 'finite' means limited (opposite to infinite). In grammar-speak it says whether a verb does (or doesn't) have a subject.

That's right. Sometimes, no one person or thing is taking the action:

> Eating my dinner
> To lie on the sand
> Writhing in pain
> Counting his money
> To sleep, to dream

We don't know who or what did any of those things.

Without a subject, they are called **non-finite** verbs.
If, however, we say this:

> I eat my dinner, lie on the sand, writhe in pain, count my money, sleep and dream.

We do know the subject. Who did those things? I did. These are called **finite verbs.**

Multi-subjects

Several verbs in a sentence can share the same subject. Often the subject is not even expressed openly. You just know it's there — it's 'understood'. The author mentioned the Witch just once in the sentence below, but inside the square brackets I've shown you that she's in fact the subject of the verb three times over.

> The Witch gave Dorothy a friendly little nod, [the Witch] whirled around on her left heel three times, and [the Witch] straightway disappeared ...

Objects

The **object** of the sentence is what's **having the action done to it**.
You locate the object by finding the verb, then asking 'whom?' or 'what?' after it.

I kicked the cat. I kicked what? *The cat.*

Australia beat Sri Lanka. Australia beat whom? *Sri Lanka.*

She loves me. She loves whom? (OK, no one would say that.) *Me.*

My dog likes bones. My dog likes what? *Bones.*

 NERD'S CORNER

Who or whom?

You could ask 'who or what?' after the verb, but strictly speaking, *whom* is correct for an object. It's like the way *he* turns into *him*, or *she* becomes *her*, depending on whether the person is the doer or the done-to. There's more on this in the section on pronouns, page 58.

Let's face it though, *whom* doesn't get a lot of use these days. It's formal, and can sound stiff. Poor old *whom* is fading out, and you can lead a perfectly happy life hardly ever using it. Just occasionally, you might need to write phrases like 'To whom it may concern', but beyond very formal writing, you shouldn't worry about it too much.

WARNING!

Singular / plural confusion

There are three major troublespots.

1. The words *each*, *every*, *either*, *neither* and *none* are singular (see page 69 for more on this), so you should say:
   - Each member of the team *is* getting a prize.
   - Neither my Mum or Dad *is* home.
   - None of us *is* going.

   The trouble is that people often do not say this, and the grammar police wouldn't even notice a plural instead of a singular verb. 'Neither my Mum or Dad are home', or 'None of us are going' can sound quite OK. I give up. I'm not going to umpire this issue. You can decide for yourself.

2. Sometimes it's hard to tell whether the subject is singular or plural. Check if the word *of* is in there somewhere. That's often the cause of the trouble.
   - A group *of* children (*is* or *are*?) visiting us today.
   - A vase *of* flowers (*make* or *makes*?) the room smell nice.

   If there's an *of* in the sentence, remove it and whatever is attached to it. It will then be easy to see if the verb should be singular or plural.
   - A vase ... *makes* the room smell nice.
   - A group ... *is* visiting us today.

3. Sometimes people just don't bother getting it right.
    - There's lots of ways ...
    - There's heaps of people ...

    THIS IS ALWAYS WRONG but you hear it all the time. Why is it wrong? Remove the apostrophe, and open the word up to its pre-condensed version. You are saying 'There *is* lots' or 'there *is* heaps'. This matches a singular verb with a plural noun. No way is that ever going to be right! You should be saying:
    - There *are* lots of ways.
    - There *are* heaps of people.

    There are plenty of examples singular / plural confusion out there in public. Here's a sign on Sydney Ferries. Which particular passenger should keep clear of the yellow zone? They should have used a plural and said 'Passengers must ...'.

> **PASSENGER MUST KEEP CLEAR OF YELLOW ZONE WHILST VESSEL IS ARRIVING OR DEPARTING THE WHARF**

Transitive and intransitive verbs

Not all verbs have objects. Verbs that do are called **transitive**, because the action transits (or travels) from the subject, through the verb, to the object. Every one of those examples above is a transitive verb. The doer does something *to* something or someone.

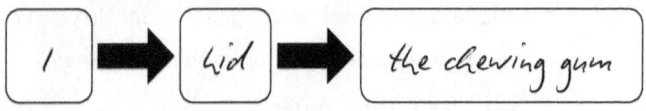

Intransitive verbs don't have an object. Some examples are *arrive, go, lie, sit, die*. There's no way to use these with an object. I can't say *I arrive you*, or *I sit it*, or *we die them*. (There's more detail about this on page 262.)

Quite a few verbs can be either transitive or intransitive, depending on how they're used.

I run.   I run marathons.

They sang.   They sang the National Anthem.

She wept.   She wept tears of joy.

Active and passive voice

The arrangement of subjects, verbs and objects has a big effect on what you say.

Imagine we're on a real soccer field in the closing minutes of a game:

> TEAM CAPTAIN: [*calling, desperate*] Marley, you missed the goal!! Now we've lost the whole season!

This is called **Active voice**. It is clear who did what. Marley is the doer and the **subject** of the verb *missed*. She missed what? *The goal*. The goal is the **object** of the verb, or the thing that the verb has been 'done to'.

Now imagine it's later, at a news conference.

> TEAM CAPTAIN: [*calm, professional*]
> Unfortunately, the goal was missed, so the season was lost.

This is called **Passive voice**. It puts the object of the sentence first. This hides the doer (the subject). We can ask 'who or what missed the goal?' and never know the answer.

Active voice is strong, simple and direct. It is clear; it hides nothing. You know who did what.

Passive voice creates a feeling of distance. It is indirect, cloudy and vague. In some situations that can be a good idea. At the news conference the team captain is nice enough not to blame Marley in public, so she tells the story in a way that makes no one in particular responsible for the loss.

Passive voice: pros and cons

I'm not a passive voice fan. When I see a notice saying 'It is a condition of entry to the store that bags are opened for inspection', I wonder why they don't just say what they mean: 'Customers must open their bags for inspection'.

It's not a bad idea to remember that distancing technique though. Saying 'mistakes were made' or 'the milk was spilled' or 'homework was forgotten' can be tactful ways of not giving someone the blame.

Some people think that passive voice sounds professional. It is expected, or even required, in some kinds of work, or academic writing. (Did you notice I just used it?) The idea is that it sounds detached and distant, more objective and less like a personal opinion. This is seen as the right tone in these contexts. Watch out for phrases like 'it can be seen that' or 'the idea has been suggested'. You will need to use them yourselves at times.

It's best for prose to be clear, active and direct – it's just easier to follow. I also can't see how concealing your opinion by using the passive voice changes the fact that it is your opinion. In my view, passive voice is best at hiding meaning, creating confusion and sounding clunky. But there are certainly times when you will be expected to use it for a certain audience.

To prove my point, look at these simple examples which rework clichés, familiar phrases and titles. Then make up your own mind.

Active voice	Passive voice
I heard it on the grapevine	It was heard on the grapevine
I will always love you	You will always be loved
I now pronounce you husband and wife	You are now pronounced husband and wife
I do solemnly swear	It is solemnly sworn
Every cloud has a silver lining	A silver lining is had by every cloud

Get good at verbs
Be thoughtful and imaginative in your choice of verbs – they are the key to great writing. It's a lot of fun to build your vocabulary using synonyms, or to play around using a thesaurus to extend the number of verbs on your personal menu. Try a word-of-the-week app, and work the new words you've discovered into what you say and write.

4
PRONOUNS

Pronouns replace nouns.

You probably use most pronouns correctly already – words like *who, what, he, she, they, themselves*. But sometimes there are tricky issues that are hard to figure out. Pronouns are one part of speech where there really are rules, and if you make a mistake you sound silly, and (more importantly) may not be understood.

Pronouns can be a bit puzzling, especially to people aged 12. It's a kind of fog in their brains. I can't explain why this is. I only know it takes a 13th birthday to clear it away. They usually 'get' pronouns after that. I hope you are either younger than 12 (fog free), or older than 13 (recovered from the condition).

Here's a chart to help you. You can see you already know these words. You may not recognise the way they are grouped. Don't worry about the headings. They will be explained as we go.

Singular			
Person	Subjective	Objective	Possessive
1st	I	me, myself	my, mine
2nd	you	you, yourself	your, yours
3rd	he, she, it	him, her, it himself, herself, itself	his, hers, its
Plural			
1st	we	us	our, ours
2nd	you	you	your, yours
3rd	they	them, themselves	their, theirs

There are three things you need to know about pronouns: what they are; what they are not; and how they work. Let's take a look.

What pronouns are

Pronouns are stand-ins. Substitutes. Pronouns are replacement words. Pronouns are used instead of nouns. Every time a person uses a pronoun, there's a noun hiding behind the pronoun.

Shall we try that again?

Pronouns are stand-ins. Substitutes. *They* are replacement words. *They* are used instead of nouns. Every time *you* use a pronoun, there's a noun hiding behind *it*. Voila! A demonstration of the pronoun *they* replacing the noun *pronouns*.

You need pronouns to avoid repeating the names of things when you speak or write. If you didn't have pronouns, things would get very dull, because repetition is boring; it slows you down and puts lumps in what you say. So pronouns smooth your language out, making it direct, sleek and easy to follow.

Sometimes a pronoun can be a useful general term that can cover for you, when you don't know the name of something.

Have a look at this passage from *Alice in Wonderland*. I have replaced the pronouns with the nouns they refer to (and underlined them).

> Either the well was very deep, or Alice fell very slowly, for <u>Alice</u> had plenty of time as <u>Alice</u> went down to look about <u>Alice</u> and to wonder <u>which thing or things</u> was going to happen next. First, <u>Alice</u> tried to look down and make out <u>which thing or things</u> <u>Alice</u> was coming to, but it was too dark to see <u>a thing of any kind</u>; then <u>Alice</u> looked at the sides of the well, and noticed that <u>the sides of the well</u> were filled with cupboards and book-shelves … <u>Alice</u> took down a jar from one of the shelves as <u>Alice</u> passed; it was labelled 'ORANGE MARMALADE', but to <u>Alice's</u> great disappointment <u>the jar</u> was empty: <u>Alice</u> did not like to drop <u>the jar</u> for fear of killing <u>some person of no known identity</u>, so managed to put <u>the jar</u> into one of the cupboards as <u>Alice</u> fell past <u>the cupboard</u>.

It's boggy. Confusing. No zing. Now try putting pronouns in place of the underlined words to convert it back to the way Lewis Carroll wrote it. When you've lost the repetitive nouns and put the pronouns back, boom! Alice falls in graceful slow motion doing things with cupboards and shelves and marmalade jars as she goes, all thanks to the pronouns *she, her, what, anything, they, it* and *somebody*.

What pronouns are not

The word *pronoun* contains the word *noun*. Therefore, some people think pronouns must be a kind of noun. Pronouns do behave like nouns, and there are grammarians who tell you that pronouns *are* a type of noun. This may be the reason for the confusion of my 12 year olds.

Because pronouns differ in so many ways from nouns, I prefer to treat them as a distinct part of speech. Believe me when I tell you:

- Pronouns are a class of their own.
- Nouns are **not** like pronouns.
- Pronouns are **not** like nouns.
- Nouns and pronouns are different.
- I cannot think of another way to say it.

How pronouns work

Pronouns replace a huge number of nouns, and there are quite a number of pronouns to do this.

While the specific noun vanishes, the pronoun that steps in still gives a bit of information about the noun that's gone missing. It's as though they have code embedded in them and can still communicate. This is useful. When Alice tumbled down the hole, the pronouns *she*, *her*, *what* (and the rest) meant we could still follow what was going on.

There are four parts to this information. Grammarians call them 'person', 'number', 'gender' and 'case'.

You know it's incorrect to say 'Her play football', but do you know why? Let's figure it out. It's all about using the right pronoun for the noun it replaces.

Person, number, gender

Check out the table on p 59. We use different pronouns depending on:

1. **Who** is talking (person).
   - If it's me (or me plus at least one other), the pronoun will be first person: *I, me, myself, we, us, ourselves, my, mine, ours.*
   - If someone is being talked to, the pronoun is second person: *you, yourself, yourselves, your, yours.*

- If we're talking about something or someone, the pronoun is third person *he, she, it, him, her, himself, herself, his, hers, its*.
2. **How many** things or people are being referred to (number). If there is only one, of course the pronoun is singular; if many, it's plural.
3. The **gender** of the original noun. If it was female, you need a feminine pronoun: *she, her, herself;* if male, you need a masculine pronoun: *he, him, himself;* and if it is neuter (no gender – a thing), you'll need *it, itself.*

Case

The fourth hidden feature of a pronoun is its case. This is about how the pronoun relates to the verb. Is it doing something, or having something done to it? Depending on the answer you will use a different pronoun.

1. 'Doers' are called **subjective** case. These pronouns are driving things. They cause the action. Because they are doers, they go before the verb. *I, you, he, she, it, we and they.*
2. The 'done to' are called **objective** case. These are on the receiving end of the action. They (usually) come after the verb: *me, myself, you, yourself, him, her, it, himself, herself* and *itself.*

To find out if the pronoun is subjective or objective, first find the verb, then ask yourself 'Is this pronoun doing this? Or having it done to them?' In our example 'Her play football', the verb is *play*. When you ask 'who is playing?' you get the answer 'her.' But because we are looking for the doer, the pronoun has to be in the subjective case. She is the player of the football. She causes the action. It has to be 'she plays football'.

If you want to replace the noun *football* with a pronoun, go through the same process. When you ask 'plays what?' you get the answer 'football'. A neuter (genderless) thing is on the receiving end of the action. You would say 'she plays it'.

3. There is a third case in English. The **possessive** case shows ownership. '*My / your / our / their* class.' Or 'That class is *mine / yours / ours / theirs*'.

Reflexive pronouns

There is one more member of the pronoun family to meet. The **reflexive pronoun** has two uses. The first is emphasis. Instead of just saying 'I taught that class', I can make more of what I have done by saying 'I taught that class myself'.

The second use of the reflexive pronoun is when the person is both the doer and the done to, both the subject and the object of the verb. We say 'I hurt myself' or 'he improved himself', not 'I hurt me' or 'he improved him'.

NERD'S CORNER

Cases?

English has only three cases: subjective, objective and possessive. These are left over from Old English, the Germanic language spoken about 1300 years ago, when Britain had been overrun by Germanic tribes.

Today, many modern languages have lots of cases, and their words change form (the technical term is 'inflect') depending on the role they perform in a sentence. In modern German there are four cases, six different words for *the* and sixteen different ways to use them, depending on the gender, person and case of the noun or pronoun that follows. Russian has eight cases and Hungarian has a whopping eighteen.

Other leftovers from Old English are the 's' we still add to make a plural noun, and the changes we make to verb endings to show person and tense: I dance, but she dances, they danced, and they're dancing.

Other case forms were mostly lost after the French-speaking Normans invaded in 1066, and English began soaking up the language of the newcomers.

Pronoun problems

Replacing yourself + 1

If you want to see an English teacher's death stare, or a red pen ready for strike action, say or write something like this:

> Jake and me are late to class because him and me were packing up.

Can you see the problem? And why it makes people like me so mad?

The difficulty here is we are often unsure how to replace **more than one noun**. Try removing one of them from the sentence. Let's drop Jake.
Is it correct to say:

> Me am late because me was packing up?

OF COURSE NOT. *Me* must not be used as a doer. You have to say '*I* arrived late because *I* was packing up'.
Now try replacing both names. Hint: you'll need a plural pronoun.
'*Jake* and *me* are late' becomes '*We* are late'.
And 'because him and me were packing up' becomes 'because *we* were packing up'.
We is the first person plural pronoun in the **subjective** case.

'Jake and *I* arrived late' or '*He* and *I* arrived late' are both grammatically correct. So are 'because Jake and *I* were packing up' and 'because *he* and *I* were packing up'.

I don't hear many people saying 'he and I' because it sounds a bit old fashioned, but it is perfectly correct when they do. No matter if there's one pronoun or two, if both parties do the action you need a **subjective** pronoun.

Now let's try it with the two of you moved to the **objective** case. Say something is being done to you.

Would you say 'We were late so the teacher gave he and I a detention'? Please don't, it is WRONGGGG.

Let's follow the same process. First remove the other person. You'd never say 'The teacher gave I a detention'. You'd say 'The teacher gave *me* a detention'. First person, singular pronoun, objective case, because something was done **to** you.

Now replace both people with one pronoun: 'The teacher gave *us* a detention'. First person, plural pronoun, **objective** case.

So once again, even when we dump just one name from the sentence, the replacement pronoun will also have to be in the objective case: 'The teacher gave Jake and me a detention'.

When both names are replaced by separate pronouns it has to be 'The teacher gave *him* and *me* a detention'. They are both in the objective case.

Part 1: Good grammar, great writing

 GIVE IT A GO

Try a few on your own. (The answers are below.)

Grandma gave Dad and I this book for Christmas.

Her and me are best friends.

Stefan, Griselda and Bo came with you and I.

The cat went up the chimney and me and my brother couldn't get her out.

Answers:

Grandma gave Dad and me this book for Christmas.

She and I are best friends.

Stefan, Griselda and Bo came with you and me.

The cat went up the chimney and I and my brother could not get her out.

Well, that's a bit awkward to say, so I guess you would say 'my brother and I'. You get the idea?

Each, Every, Either, Neither, None

On page 52 we said that these are always singular, because they refer to just one item. Sure, the one item is part of a larger group, but you are talking about just one member so singular verbs are correct.

However, using the singular pronoun can sound stilted, and a lot of people will not be concerned to hear plural pronouns used in these situations.

Here are some examples:

- Each / Every team member *is* getting an award for *his* or *her* work. (Or should it be '*their* work'?)
- Each / Every teacher has been to university for *his* or *her* degree. (Or should it be '*their* degree'?)
- Each / Every citizen *has* one vote to use as *they* choose. (Or should it be 'as *he* or *she* chooses'?)

You will have to decide for yourself / yourselves.

He, She, They

You don't see this much anymore, but there was a time when the pronoun *he* was used to mean a group of men and women. You might have heard the word *mankind*. It's the same idea – *man* is used to mean *human*. These days when we want a group pronoun we usually use *they*, *them* or *their*. Even though it's plural, we let it stand in for a singular noun that can include any gender.

If *your child* wants dessert *they* can come and get it now.

A teacher must be fair when *they* grade *their* students' work.

Between you and I, it is I

There is a whole world of pronoun 'mistakes' that fussy people like to correct. In my opinion they are showing off. Common examples are the phrases 'between you and I', and 'it is me'. Believe it or not, these are technically *in*correct. This is to do with old-fashioned rules that I will now explain, briefly, so I don't put you to sleep.

The word *between* is a **preposition** (see pages 79–83) and the pronouns that prepositions govern are always meant to be in the objective case. Who knows why. It's therefore correct to say 'between you and *me*' rather than 'between you and *I*', because *me* is the objective case.

I suspect the reason 'between you and I' has become so common is that children are taught to say 'you and I' to be polite. You say 'you and I' if the rest of the sentence is 'are having lunch / playing handball / standing on our heads' because it's courteous to put yourself last. The trouble is it just isn't the right form when 'between' or any other preposition is the starting point of the sentence.

As to the second phrase, 'it is me', if you read the section on verb complements on page 262, you'll learn the verb 'to be' is very special. It never takes the objective case. It follows that if someone asks 'Who's there?' you should answer 'It is I'.

Well, please go ahead. You may be grammatically correct but you will sound really weird. Hardly anyone talks that way nowadays and neither should you. My rule of thumb in these cases is to say what sounds normal.

Cohesion

This means 'unity' or 'sticking together'. If your pronouns are not perfect, your prose will come unstuck. The most common cause of 'cohesion confusion' is when a pronoun could relate to more than one noun. It makes the meaning impossible to understand.

Let's say you get this text message:

> I don't feel like it but I'll see you at training.

Does your friend not feel like seeing you? Or do they not feel like training? The confusion is because the pronoun *it* could refer to either of those. We can't tell what this person means.

Always check that pronouns are not hanging loose and unattached. And feel free to join the Grammar Police and hunt these villains down. We need to put an end to their devious deceptions, so we can be properly understood!

Narrative voice

Pronouns are vital to good writing. They provide the **narrative voice**, which is also called perspective, or **point of view**.

Lewis Carroll has Alice tumbling down a hole. He uses the pronouns *she* and *her* to tell us about it, so we say this is a **third person narrative voice**.

> Either the well was very deep, or *she* fell very slowly, for *she* had plenty of time as *she* went down to look about *her* and to wonder what was going to happen next.

Writing in the third person is extremely common. Read a novel recently? Who told the story? Chances are it was written in the third person. It works like a kind of all-seeing eye, called an **omniscient narrator**. An invisible storyteller knows everything that's going on, and can read the minds and the thoughts, and sense the feelings, and know all the actions of all the characters in the story.

They can tell us where they went, how they felt, what they said, and what they ate for breakfast.

Imagine instead Lewis Carroll used *I*. Alice would be telling the story herself. In that case we'd say the narrative voice is in the **first person**.

> Either the well was very deep, or *I* fell very slowly, for *I* had plenty of time as *I* went down to look about *me* and to wonder what was going to happen next.

When you tell a story in the first person you own it. It sounds personal. Saying 'I' makes it sincere and believable. You always use the first person for a diary, or a memoir, or recounting some experience that you had. You can also use it in an opinion piece, or a persuasive essay. If you want to make a story sound immediate, as if it's happening right now, combine first person pronouns with the present tense.

> I slide down from my bunk and pull on my pants, a sweatshirt and a cap. I yank my boots on. In the bowl by the sink are two apples. I pick up both, and as the screen door slams behind me I bite into one.

The trouble with a first person account is that it means we see things through just one angle. That's not always desirable.

GIVE IT A GO

There's a lot of difference between first- and third-person narratives. It's a good exercise to switch the point of view. What does an incident look like if someone else is telling it? What changes does that create?

Rewrite the story of *Goldilocks and the Three Bears*, first told by the bears, and then by Goldilocks. Each will be quite a different tale, and you will definitely need a lot of first-person pronouns in both cases: 'I' and 'We'.

Make sure you don't switch between the first and the third person by accident! That's sloppy and will not impress your reader.

5
ADVERBS

The adverb does what its name says. It *adds* to a *verb*.

I'd like it if the sentence above was true, but it isn't quite. Adverbs are a broad and capable group. As well as adding to verbs, they can get to work on other adverbs, adjectives, noun phrases, clauses and whole sentences.

Adverbs often end in 'ly', but not always. (I could just as easi*ly* have said they usual*ly*, or frequent*ly*, end in 'ly', to prove my point.)

Like adjectives, adverbs are called **modifiers** or **qualifiers**.

You can add also *more* or *most* to some adverbs to make a comparison.

Four types of adverbs

There are four types of adverbs. In grammar-speak we call them adverbs of *time*, *manner*, *degree* and *place*.

They tell us, when, how, to what degree and where.

Some adverbs of degree are known as 'limiters' because they build a kind of fence around something, saying how far it goes. Examples are *only, almost, just, nearly* and *hardly*.

> I ride my bike *daily* (time / when), *everywhere* (place / where), and *quite* (degree) *carefully* (manner / how).
>
> I *only* (degree / limiter) have classes *near* (place) home *today* (time), *annoyingly* (manner).
>
> She's a *very* (degree) tall girl and *regularly* (time) plays *almost* (degree) professional basketball *very well* (degree, manner).

Limiters go right in front of the word they modify, but other adverbs can go pretty well anywhere, depending on what makes sense and sounds good. This can lead to confusion, though, so be careful that you say what you mean to say.

The **misplaced modifier** is a writing blooper – an adverb floating about in the wrong place makes your meaning unclear. Have a look at these. There's just no way to tell what they mean. The adverb is in a place that makes the sentence completely ambiguous.

> I agreed *after* the show to meet you and go home.

Am I meeting you after the show? Or was it after the show when we made the agreement? Search me.

> I *only* walk to school on Tuesdays.

Do you use other types of transport as well as walking on the other days? Or do you walk to school just once a week, on Tuesdays? I don't know because the adverb is misplaced.

Writing well with adverbs

Adverbs add an extra layer of meaning to a verb, and that's what we want them to do. Use them for light and shade, for nuance. For instance, I could breathe *slowly* or *rhythmically* or *haltingly*. Depending which adverb I choose, I'm saying something slightly different. My slow breathing might be because I'm controlling my temper; my rhythmic breathing might be because I'm exercising at a comfortable pace; and if I'm breathing haltingly I'm probably struggling to get my breath. Perhaps I've had a shock, or am puffed and trying to speak while gasping for air.

It's providing these subtle shades of meaning that an adverb does best.

Most good writers tell you that if you choose all your other words well you don't need many adverbs. I agree up to a point. The fuss about adverbs is mostly aimed at the 'ly' words. It's that pesky last syllable that makes a sentence sound bulked up and tangled. I usually cut the words ending in 'ly' in anything I write, but that's because I overuse them – maybe you don't.

The 'ly' words leak in to our writing because we use them all the time when we speak. *Actually*, *suddenly*, *hopefully*, *currently*, *certainly* and *incredibly* are *really* common in conversation. They're also big players in clichés. They make up half the phrases we use *thoughtlessly* all the time. Everyone falls *hopelessly* in love, stares *blankly* into space, sleeps *fitfully* or *soundly* or *hardly* a wink, has friends who are *really* cool, and parents who are *really* mean. These all deserve the chop, but you do need adverbs of time and place because you must say when and where things happen. And limiters are vital to being accurate in your descriptions.

In summary? Use adverbs by all means, but be sure they add value.

WISE ADVICE

A little goes a long way
Don't overdo them. Some adverbs double up on their verb mates and don't add much meaning. There's no need to 'whisper *quietly*' or 'creep *stealthily*'. The verb captures that idea by itself.

It's also worth taking the scissors to *very*, *really* and *quite*, which are top of the 'uselessly overused' list. Where's the point in saying 'I hit the bullseye *very* accurately'? Or 'I dawdled *really* slowly'? Or 'I *quite* agree'. It's just filling in space.

6
PREPOSITIONS

I love these little guys. They are *locator* words. The clue is right there in the name: prePOSITION. A preposition adds a sense of where or when. They connect things, create relationships. Prepositions are always followed by a noun or pronoun.

There are only about 150 of them. Most are teeny weeny words, but they are powerful drivers of meaning. *Of, to, for* and *in* are among the top ten most used words in English, and they are prepositions. *On, by, near, off, on, up, down, over, under, beside, behind, beneath, below, within, beyond* and *towards* are all prepositions. We need them if we are looking for something.

Ago, after, before, during, since, until, when, about and *throughout* are prepositions that help us locate things in time.

We aren't really inventing new prepositions any more. Some grammarians say they're a 'closed group'. A club that's not accepting any new members. If we are not making up new prepositions, it means the ones we've got are quite stable and have retained their meaning through the centuries.

Hard-working, flexible little words

They have little meaning on their own, yet in a sentence, prepositions can change everything. Let's say there's a princess *in* a castle. How much does that change when she's *near, around, beneath, behind, outside* or *by* the castle? A lot. Thank you, prepositions. If you change nothing but the preposition, you get a completely different sentence.

Try it:

The letter was written by me.

Which word shows that I did the writing? Easy: *by*. In what other very obvious way could I have been connected to the writing, and what word would show that? Yesss! The letter was written *to* me. New preposition – new meaning.

I was injured by the ball in a game of cricket.

Which word tells you the ball caused my injury? *By*. And which word tells you I'm a cricketer? *In*. What could you change that to if I was a spectator? *At*.

They're going to Melbourne.

Which word shows that Melbourne is the destination? *To*. What preposition would reverse the meaning? *From*.

There's a vase of roses on the table.

How are the vase and the table related? Which word shows this? *On.* What other prepositions could you use to show a different relationship between the vase and the table? *Under, near, by* ...

Same word, different meaning

One problem with prepositions is that the same word can mean different things in different situations. Like so many English words, it all depends on context, or what's being talked about. I'm told there are at least eighteen ways to use *at*. (Want to try?)

If you're at the beach you might say 'I'm going in'. You run down and get into the water. After a few minutes swimming out beyond the breakers, you look back at the beach and say 'I'm going in'. You mean the exact opposite of what you meant the last time you said it. Crazy. My guess is that we say we go *in* to shore because it's opposite to *out* to sea, but we get *in* to water – pools, puddles, rivers, baths, oceans – because, well, we just do. Somehow the two got mixed up. Who knows. My point is, you must know the context to understand either sentence correctly.

Crucially, prepositions are often linked to certain nouns or adjectives. They work as a pair and can't be disconnected. It's as if they are married and cannot be divorced. These two linked words are called a **prepositional phrase**.

Consider the noun *time*. We can use at least eight prepositions with it: *in* time, *on* time, *out of* time, *behind* time, *through* time, *under* time or *over* time.

How about the noun *work*? I can be *at* work, *in* work, or looking *for* work if I am *out of* work. I can even be *over* work when I've had enough of it. Each preposition changes the meaning of the phrase completely, while the noun sits there and does nothing. If you use the wrong preposition in any of these situations, it will get you into trouble, and you won't be understood.

It's infuriating (but typical of English) that the opposite is also true. Some prepositions *can* be swapped and substituted. I can be *in* a shop or *at* a shop, working *at* home or *from* home, *in* the team or *on* the team. I say I am bored *with* something, and young people often say they're bored *of* something. This looks like it's changing, but whichever preposition I choose my meaning will be clear.

There are also geographical and historical variations. In Australia, we're supposed to say *different from* and not *different to*. (My Mum's been ticking me off for that since I had pigtails.) In the USA, people say different *than*. In the USA you say a house is *on* a street, but in Australia and Britain it's *in* the street. In Australia and Britain we wait *in* line but in some parts of the USA it's *on* line.

You cannot guess the correct preposition to use; you just have to know which one is right. Make a mistake and you may not be understood.

Prepositions and the objective case

You will notice, if you stop and think about it, that pronouns following a preposition are always in the objective case (see page 70). Come to the movies *with me*? Stand *by her*! Please hold the umbrella *over them*. I was *before him* in the queue. We say that the preposition **governs** the pronoun.

> **NERD'S CORNER**
>
> ### Sentences ending with a preposition
> There's a – frankly – ridiculous idea that you shouldn't end a sentence with a preposition. It is something 'up with which I cannot put', as Winston Churchill supposedly said. He didn't mean it. He was poking fun at how silly that sentence sounds.
>
> If you tried to do this you wouldn't be able to say ordinary things like 'What are you laughing at?', 'When's the assignment due by?', 'Who are you going out with?', 'That's the place we're staying at' or 'There's a lot to complain about'.
>
> It's an out-of-date rule that was once taught to schoolchildren because Latin works that way. A modern English speaker can basically forget it, unless you want to spend your life saying things like 'At what are you laughing?', 'By when must I complete my assignment?' or 'There's a lot about which to complain'.
>
> Your English teacher may set a test question that asks something like 'For what words is each of these synonyms used?' – but really, all these examples sound so complicated and clunky, you can see why I say 'Not happening!'

7
ARTICLES

The little words *the, a* and *an* are called articles. They all go before a noun. *The* is called the **definite article** because it is – well, definite. It's for a specific thing: '*the* ball'. *A* and *an* are **indefinite articles** because they're non-specific: '*a* ball'. Any old ball. *An* is always used before a noun that starts with a vowel, just to make it easier to say: 'an answer'.

Other words that do a similar job include **possessives** (*my, her, your, its, our*) and **demonstratives** (*this, that, these, those*). These are usually called **determiners**.

8
CONJUNCTIONS

Conjunctions are the 'joining' or 'connector' words that allow you to expand your sentences to include more than one idea. The best-known conjunctions are *and* and *but*, but there are loads more. (It was fun repeating *and* and *but* like that – you don't normally get to do it.)

Three types of joining words

Grammarians have divided conjunctions into three groups.

1 **Co-ordinating** conjunctions connect two equal things (words, phrases or clauses). The most common ones are *and, but, or, nor, yet* and *so*.
2 **Subordinating** conjunctions link two *un*equal words, phrases or clauses. They work to link a main idea to a supporting idea. It's a sort of up / down relationship. (There's more about this in the section on clauses on page 132.) They let you

know that what comes next is extra information. It's not the main idea.

Common subordinating conjunctions are *because, although, though, since, as, if, however* and *while*. Other useful ones are *that, than, till, unless, until, when, whenever, where* and *whether or not*.

As we know, sometimes words that are normally one part of speech can act like another. Adverbs like *until, after* and *before* can also work as conjunctions: 'I laughed until my ribs ached'. In English it all depends on context.

3 **Correlative** conjunctions are pairs of words (or phrases) that work together.
either ... or
neither ... nor
not only ... but also
both ... and
so ... as
whether ... or

That word *correlative* is going out of fashion and these are not always seen as a separate group.

Conjunctions in action

Let's see a few:

> I dropped French [*as* I wasn't enjoying it].

The main idea is that you dropped French. Using *as* tells us the rest adds more information about why you did so.

> [*Because* we were running late,] we took a taxi *and* arrived on time.

And is a co-ordinator, so it suggests (indirectly) that it's of equal importance that you took a taxi and arrived on time. The subordinating conjunction *Because* leads into some extra information – the reason you took the taxi in the first place.

Let's change that sentence to:

> We were running late *so* we took a taxi *and* arrived on time.

We now have all three ideas joined by co-ordinating conjunctions, which means all three are equally important.

Writing well with conjunctions

You should love conjunctions because they extend your sentences. They gain length. Your writing becomes flexible and plastic. These are the words that help make your prose flow. Conjunctions give you control over a sentence's shape, pace and movement. In school this might be called *cohesion*.

You're unlikely to make a mistake and use a wrong conjunction. It's more a matter of choosing ones that work well. How do you want your sentences to sound? What's your style? You must make sure your meaning is clear and your ideas are connected smoothly.

The risk is that you'll use too many of the simple ones. Many young writers come up with stories that are just a list, joined together by *and*:

> We went to school *and* we learned writing *and* we had recess *and* played games *and* we did spelling *and* we went out to lunch *and* played games *and* then we went home.

It's repetitive and boring.

The word *and* is a bit like a plus sign. Very simple. However, you do need it if you want to make lists. If you want to avoid repetition, you need other conjunctions and other arrangements. Variety is, as they say, the spice of life. It's also the way to get good marks.

Suppose we rearrange it a bit:

> We went home *after* a day at school *where* we learned spelling and writing, *and* played games at lunch and recess.

It's more enjoyable to read, don't you think?

Cohesion (again)

Conjunctions are essential for creating connections.

Look at this sentence from *Dr Doolittle*, by Hugh Lofting. The author has five things to list, and he wants to say two things about each: what they are and where they are. That's ten things! But it never feels like a boring ten-item list. That's because he only uses two conjunctions, and one of them is at the start of the sentence. He separates the rest using commas, so we don't get bored.

> *Besides* the gold-fish in the pond at the bottom of his garden, [Dr Doolittle] had rabbits in the pantry, white mice in his piano, a squirrel in the linen closet *and* a hedgehog in the cellar.

Opening with *Besides the gold-fish*, gives Dr Doolittle a certain comic charm. As the list grows we start to smile at his silliness.

If he'd written this, however –

> Dr Doolittle had gold-fish in the pond at the bottom of his garden, and rabbits in the pantry, and white mice in his piano, and a squirrel in the linen closet, and a hedgehog in the cellar.

– it would feel ploddy and dull.

There's a fancy term for using lots of co-ordinating conjunctions to create a deliberate stylistic effect. It's called *polysyndeton*. I don't recommend it!

In this next version there are no conjunctions. See how this changes the way the writing flows. Without conjunctions we can only write short, snappy sentences that sound like gunfire. I think this gives the idea that Dr Doolittle is irritating, and the writer is impatient with him. There are just too many animals to take seriously. I almost expect the next sentence to be 'And it had to be stopped!'

> Dr Doolittle had gold-fish in the pond at the bottom of his garden. He had rabbits in the pantry, he had white mice in his piano. He had a squirrel in the linen closet. He also had a hedgehog in the cellar.

If you're showing off, this absence of conjunctions is called *asyndeton*.

Conjunctions are also important because they help you hold on to a number of storylines at once. With conjunctions you can stretch a sentence out and send it up a hill and back down again, or take a turn around the block before coming back to the path you were on in the first place. With conjunctions, you can move something into the shadows and bring it back to the sunlight.

Here's *Alice in Wonderland* again. It's the scene where she has been playing croquet with a flamingo as a mallet and a hedgehog as the ball.

> Alice thought she might as well go back, and see how the game was going on, as she heard the Queen's voice in the distance, screaming with passion. She had already heard her sentence three of the players to be executed for having missed their turns, and she did not like the look of things at all, as the game was in such confusion that she never knew whether it was her turn or not. So she went in search of her hedgehog.

This paragraph has only three sentences. Yet it strings together information about the Queen, Alice's mood and the way the croquet game is going. That's three storylines, linked using six conjunctions. Notice that the last sentence starts with a conjunction, and is much shorter than the previous two. It's a neat conclusion to the paragraph.

But can a sentence start with 'and' or 'but'?

Schoolchildren down the ages have been taught that it's wrong to start a sentence with *and* or *but*. That's wrong. A whole bookshelf of very respectable authorities have always said that this rule is nonsense. And great writers do it all the time, so why shouldn't you?

I bet you won't even notice the sentence-starting conjunctions here, so I've underlined them:

> <u>So</u> [Alice] set the little [pig] down, and felt quite relieved to see it trot away … '<u>If</u> it had grown up,' she said to herself, 'it would have made a dreadfully ugly child. <u>But</u> it makes rather a handsome pig …'. <u>And</u> she began thinking over other children she knew, who might do very well as pigs …

Nothing wrong with that! There's no other way to get the same effect.

Perhaps teachers have just grown bored with the repetitive use of *and* in their students' work. Instead of banning it as a sentence-starter, they'd be better off teaching their kids how to start their sentences with interest. That's the real skill a writer needs.

There is no reason to avoid *and* or *but* at the start of a sentence, except if it doesn't sound good.

{PART 2}

ESSENTIAL SKILLS FOR WRITING WELL

HERE'S WHAT YOU NEED TO DO

This part of the book looks at the technical skills you need to write well. Much as you need to practise scales to play an instrument, and to work out regularly to stay fit, there are basic skills which underpin your writing. Here they come.

1
SPELLING

Spelling is the bridge between the spoken and the written word. It's how we convert one into the other.

All children learn to speak as a normal part of growing. You start with gurgling *mama dada* sounds, then you move on to baby talk, and eventually you can make complete, meaningful utterances. It just happens naturally, like getting two sets of teeth (not at the same time!), and learning to sit, crawl and walk.

That's not true for reading and writing. These have to be learned.

Learning spelling starts at an early age. Most of what you need to know was locked and loaded into your neural pathways long before you started reading this.

Learning to spell

To be able to spell, you must break into a word and understand its parts. You are like a surgeon, opening a patient up in order to examine what's inside. Pulling a word to pieces helps you figure out which letters could be used to make its different sounds, and also what the word might mean. If you meet a new word you can work out what sounds those written letters might make.

Without realising it, a good speller is aware of a word's:
- sound (phonics)
- appearance (graphics – the letters used)
- meaning and 'family' relationships (connections to other words with related meanings)
- origins (etymology – how the word got to us).

About 10% of English words these days are not spelled the way they sound. Think about it. By now you automatically know that 'ph' sounds the same as 'f', and that the 'k' in 'kn' is silent. You know that 'ough' has lots of pronunciation possibilities; the suffix 'ed' shows past tense and the 'e' is usually silent; the prefixes 'un' and 'anti' usually turn a word into its opposite, and so on.

Let's be honest – English spelling is a mess. There's almost no point in learning 'rules' for spelling because so many of them are breakable.

It's because modern English is a rich brew, developed from a mash-up of other languages. We have imported foreign (there's one!) words and spellings, and we've changed the way words sound over time, while the spelling stayed the same. The result is a whole pile of inconsistencies, and that's what causes the confusion. Just look at this:

> I drank champagne with a charming bachelor who came by parachute.

'C' and 'k' are both there, making the same sound. And as for the 'ch' combination ...

All those *ch* words have a French connection. The hard 'ch' (as in *ch*arming ba*ch*elor) is in the words that got here several hundred years ago. The *ch* pronounced as *shh* (*ch*ampagne, para*ch*ute) are more recent arrivals. They haven't shed their 'Frenchness' yet.

Seven sources of spelling confusion

If spelling challenges you, it might help to see a list of what you're up against.

1 One letter can make different sounds: fl*a*t, st*a*r, *a*ny, *a*bout.
2 Pairs and clusters of letters can look alike but sound different: dinos*aur*, l*augh*, m*auve*.

3   The same sound can be made by different letters and letter clusters: *g*inger, *j*oke, e*dge*, ca*ge*.
4   The same letter cluster can be pronounced in many different ways: there are nine (yes, nine) different ways to pronounce ough: cough, enough, plough, dough. You can find the rest for yourselves.
5   Words can be spelled differently but sound the same: *base, bass*.
6   Words can sound different but be spelled the same: *bow* (hair), *bow* (fold yourself over); *desert* (leave), *desert* (very dry region where you should not go alone).
7   Silent letters. Lots of these. For example: the 'h' in 'wh' (*which, what*); the 'b' in *comb, lamb, limb*; the 'u' in *guitar, guess, guest*; the 'w' in *wrap, write, wrong*, to name just a few.

Silent letters are responsible for some of the craziest spellings we have in English: *aisle, eight, would, yolk, yacht, gnash, receipt, debt, island*. Google 'why is English spelling so weird?' for more on this, and if you want to while away a wet afternoon, look at the Online Eymology Dictionary: www.etymonline.com. You can read the history and relationships of all these crazies and discover why they are spelled that way. It's interesting.

Silly sentences to prove the point

How many examples of the seven sources of confusion can you find in these sentences?

> I learned the list by rote then wrote it, but I didn't write it right.
>
> Few people knew that the feud was over a pool cue.
>
> We asked if we could lessen the lesson time, but the Principal said no on principle.
>
> The coward cowered, 'Don't desert me here in the desert! I'm too weak to last the week!'
>
> 'Certainly sir, suit yourself,' said the tailor to Mr Taylor, 'but there's sure a surge of interest in serge suits'.
>
> We've sold the shoes you wanted soled.
>
> You might have died or lost an eye trying to ride at that frightening height.

Spelling for success

When it comes to quality writing you are judged by how well you spell.

Please don't worry if you have trouble with spelling. Many people do. There *are* certain patterns, and there *are* clues inside some words that will help you. It is, however, mostly a memory game. If it's not easy for you, you will have to do some work or get some help. Believe me: it's worth it in the long run.

Most markers will accept minor errors in complex or challenging words, but in truth there's a zero-tolerance policy for misspelling. *All* words have to be correct.

You will boost your prestige and improve your marks by using difficult words and spelling them properly. This means, of course, that you need a strong vocabulary. More on that in the next section.

What goes wrong

When you learn to spell words in lists, or for a spelling bee, you may not really help yourself learn to use those words. Words don't work in isolation – they need an operating context. You need to put them into action to learn them properly.

Lots of people get words right in a spelling test, but they don't spot mistakes when they are writing on their own. You might spell *burglar* correctly in a test, but ten minutes later write *burgular* in a paragraph! Worse, you mightn't notice the mistake in the flow of the prose – which just shows you hadn't really learned the word.

How to put it right

To improve your spelling, you must do more than memorise the letters. You have to put the word into action by using it to express yourself.

You probably learned spelling using the 'look, say, cover, write' method, which is effective because it involves a range of different sensory and motor skills to help the word lodge in your brain.

You will greatly improve your spelling if you add a further step and **use the word in a creative sentence**. Make an effort with these sentences. Let's say the word is *banish* – don't just take the easy option and write 'I banish you!' Be creative and try a bit harder; let your imagination loose, make a longer sentence. It's more fun to come up with something like this:

> 'Banish all thoughts of failure!' she said to herself at the top of the ski run.

Finding words to work on

The first step is to make up your own personal spelling book. Write the words you get wrong into a book and then learn them using 'look, cover, say, write, USE' (I added the last bit because I know it works).

The internet is alive with spelling lists, so long as you know what to look for. Here's a list of useful search terms. Take care that they fit your age group, and see if they are suitable for your particular problem. If the words on the list are too simple, or so unfamiliar that you would not be likely to use them, keep searching.

Look for lists of:

- most commonly used words in English
- frequently misspelled words
- words with silent letters in them
- etymologies (word origins)
- prefixes and suffixes
- homophones (words that are spelled differently, but sound the same)

 NERD'S CORNER

The history of crazy spelling

Professor Penny Gay of the English Department at the University of Sydney explains it for us: 'There are many hand-written examples of Old, Middle and Early Modern English with individual spellings, often due to local dialects and pronunciations. The first printed books in English date from the 15th century, and the first dictionaries (or 'word-lists') came in the later 16th century. But spelling wasn't in any way regularised. Also at this time, lots and lots of ballad-sheets, poems and plays were printed, all with different spelling patterns, according to the taste of the person in the printing-house who set them. Spelling really only settled into something that looks more modern in the late 17th century, and with the rise in cheap novels, newspapers and magazines that took place at the beginning of the 18th century. The appearance of *Johnson's Dictionary* in 1755 was the biggest influence in settling the spelling of most words.'

Part 2: Essential skills for writing well

- words relating to different subject areas
- digraphs and blends (two or more letters making one sound).

Spelling on the move

It's good fun to look at the spelling in texts written a long time ago to see some of the ways pronunciation changes over time. What once was a rhyme isn't always a rhyme any more. A famous poem by William Blake called 'The Tyger' (nowadays often 'The Tiger') has the following two lines in it:

> What immortal hand or eye
> Could frame thy fearful symmetry?

You can tell right away that either *eye* or *symmetry* must have been pronounced differently when Blake wrote that poem.

The reverse is also true. Spelling could change while pronunciation didn't. It's well known that Shakespeare spelled his name in at least six different ways. I'm guessing he always pronounced it the same way though.

Have you noticed the way spelling is changing with technology? Thanks to the smartphone, texting is now the main form of informal written communication. I don't think many of us care too much about correct spelling in texts anymore. We abbreviate and use shortcuts all the time. Do you imagine we will go back to the spell-it-anyhow-you-like-so-long-as-it-makes-sense days? And should we?

Personal bloopers

Most people know some words only by sight, not sound, and vice versa. So we mentally decide on our own ways of spelling or sounding them, and we can easily make a mistake.

I spent my childhood thinking the written word *misled* was pronounced 'my-sld', the past tense of a mysterious verb *misle*. I also knew and used the word *mis-led* (as in 'she misled me by lying'), but I didn't realise this was how it was spelled. I obviously never looked it up or I'd have discovered my mistake!

My friend thought there was a country called 'Eggy-put', and didn't realise it was the same place she knew as 'Egypt'. She also thought that *bedraggled* meant how you looked when you got out of bed: 'bed-raggled'.

Ask someone you know to confess their personal bloopers. It's often very funny.

2
VOCABULARY

To be a good writer, a good talker or, for that matter, an interesting person, you need a good vocabulary. Choosing the right word for the job can make you sound like a genius, a poet, an expert, a dope, a friend, a comfort, maybe even an opponent or an enemy. It's all in the words you use.

Words never work independently. They have to be put together and mixed up to create an effect. If words were food, they'd be like the separate ingredients for a tasty meal. They are not the meal itself.

However, having good ingredients is an important part of creating that tasty meal.

Word families

As we know already, English words belong to families, just like me and you. They have ancestors, and connections and relationships to each other.

You can normally recognise a 'word family' because there's something similar or repetitive about its members.

They have a common base. Just as you and your cousins all have big noses or long feet, words share a common pattern of spelling or syllables. When you understand how to use the word *depend*, you are also clued in to the meaning of *dependable*, *dependent* and *independent*. These connections are easy to see and the meaning is not too hard to figure out.

Prefixes and suffixes

Very many English words started out as Greek or Latin words. Try Googling 'List of Greek and Latin roots'. You'll find Wikipedia has hundreds of entries. In fact these Greek and Latin words are so ubiquitous (look it up!) that you may not have even noticed their presence.

In the early years of school you would have learned to recognise root words, prefixes and suffixes. This is important for understanding how a word is put together. That in turn helps you figure out what a new word might mean.

A *sub*marine is a vessel that goes under the water; *sub*merge is also to go under water; *sub*stratum is a layer inside the Earth. Guess what? The prefix *sub* means 'under' and it comes to us from Latin.

Tele is Greek and it means 'far'. That explains *tele*vision, *tele*scope, *tele*phone – and a recent arrival, *tele*porting.

What about *anti*? Also Greek. It means 'against'. Let me introduce *anti*biotic, *ant*agonise, *anti*septic, *anti*bacterial. Also *anti*freeze, *anti*social and *anti*perspirant.

How about *bi*? Greek for 'two', leading to *bi*cycle, *bi*focals, *bi*nary, *bi*sect and *bi*lingual.

Bio is the Greek word for 'life', which gives us *bio*logical, *bio*graphy and sym*bio*sis.

Making new words

Prefixes and suffixes are used to create new words. When you go to the doctor, you're a patient. When you go into hospital, you're an *in*patient. If you visit a clinic at the hospital and go home again, you are an *out*patient.

If you know that *mis* is a prefix that turns things into their opposite, and you meet the word *misdirect*, assuming you already know what *direct* means, you have no problem understanding it. Likewise *misinform*, *mislead*, *misspell* and so on.

If you know what *fight* means, you'll easily understand *fighter*; *train* gives you *trainer*; and *sail* gets you to *sailor* despite the spelling change.

Building vocabulary

In the section on spelling we learned about using words in context. Vocabulary also has to be learned in context. Therefore, reading is an important activity. By encountering new words you'll learn what they mean, and see how to use them because of the situation in which you found them.

Using new words is also important. To make your own writing better, you need to employ the words that you've learned and put them to work in a new situation that you have created.

Here are a few more ways to develop your vocabulary:

- Play word games like hangman, Scrabble, wordfinders, Dictionaries, Bananagrams.
- Rustle up a 'synonym storm' or have an 'antagonistic antonym' competition; compete to think of as many similar or opposite words as you can.
- Go to an online thesaurus or Google 'Other ways to say' to locate words you find exciting, interesting or 'different'. Work them into your writing. (Be careful not to sound like you swallowed the dictionary. You still need to sound like YOU.)
- Use a 'word of the week' app.

3
PUNCTUATION

We need punctuation to bridge the gap between the spoken and the written word. When we speak we have a voice, a face and a body to add meaning to what we say. These are not available to us in writing.

A voice works like a paintbrush; it helps create a mood and a message.

Think of all the ways your mum can say your name. Just by varying her voice in speaking that one word, she can let you know that she's pleased, or cross, that you're in danger, that something nice is about to happen or that she wants to get your attention.

You can speak rapidly, making yourself sound urgent and excited, or angry or frustrated. Or you can speak slowly, making yourself sound deliberate, or careful, or (just possibly) stupid. You can stress a word to give it emphasis, and you raise the pitch of your voice to ask a question or show surprise or shock – to name just a few emotional possibilities.

When speaking to each other, we can pause and have a think. We can wait to see the response we're getting before we carry on. We have a whole body that can be used to show something without saying it, by pointing or looking, shrugging or using all sorts of other gestures.

And what about facial expressions? You can tell by looking at someone whether they're being funny or serious, whether they're upset or puzzled, or in one of a million other moods.

Why we need to punctuate

When language is written down, all those expressive possibilities are lost. Vocal variation, body language and facial expression are just not there in written form. How on earth are we going to replace them and get what they do onto a page? We punctuate!

Punctuation helps you to interpret how writing *should* sound.

Those squiggles and dots are code. They say 'this is what you would do with your voice here', and in that way they give you the direction you need to convert the written word into the spoken word (even though it's only being spoken inside your head).

You already know that punctuation can completely change the meaning of a sentence. It's just a comma, but there's a huge difference between saying 'Let's eat, Grandpa' and 'Let's eat Grandpa'. Only one of them is going to make Grandpa happy.

Or try this: 'We ate, Grandpa', or 'We ate Grandpa!'

The comma in the first one makes us pause. It tells us we are speaking to Grandpa. The meaning is 'We've eaten our meal without you'. The exclamation mark at the end of the second one tells us the mood is not calm. Excited, frantic, alarmed ... 'Oh no, we've eaten Grandpa! how did that happen?' See how punctuation completely changes the meaning?

 NERD'S CORNER

Early forms of punctuation

Back in the very old days of ancient Greece, dramatists would put marks on the text to help actors in a play know how to speak it aloud: what to stress, where to pause and so on. In fact, actors still do this. It's called marking your script. In the Middle Ages, when few people could read, and the Bible was read aloud or sung, there were also marks on the text to guide the singers or speakers to pause and use emphasis correctly. These old marks are the ancestors of our modern-day punctuation.

Five groups of squiggly marks

You might have got a fright if I'd told the truth in that heading. In fact, there are twelve common punctuation marks in English. They fall into five groups, but a proficient punctuator needs control over twelve possible signs.

You are going to look sloppy if you don't use them correctly. You will definitely lose marks in exams. You have quite a bit of freedom to use some punctuation marks as a matter of your personal style, but their correct use is not negotiable.

Stop it!

The way you end a sentence conveys meaning. There are three punctuation marks just for that.

- **Full stop** – that small dot at the bottom of your script (known in America as a **period**) is the heavyweight of punctuation. Do not fight with this guy. A full stop is definite. No discussion. This is finished.
- **Question mark** – you know how you lift the pitch of your voice toward the end of a question? That's how we know it's a question. If you don't lift your voice you're making a statement. In the written version, you need the little hook shaped squiggle with a dot so readers know that you're asking something.
- **Exclamation mark** – is a way of expressing strong feeling. Perhaps it's excitement, or outrage, shock or joy. Whatever … This end mark has some 'pow' in it.

We are seeing a lot more use of exclamation marks since email and smartphones made it easy for us to 'talk' to each other in real-time rapid writing. These days an exclamation mark in an informal communication can just show a positive feeling. 'See you soon!' shows that you're looking forward to it. In non-personal writing, for example at school, it's best to save these for sentences that really do show strong feeling.

Slow down

Suppose you don't want to stop altogether. There are six ways to slow things down in your writing. Most are familiar, but some have a few tricks for you to master. Here we go.

Commas

- **Commas** are a sort of 'half ending'. They slow you down but they don't stop you. A comma doesn't put an end to a sentence. Its job is to separate parts of a sentence to allow a reader to pause, or digest the idea just expressed.

    I went for an early run, and had breakfast when I got home.

    That sentence contains two related ideas, with a break between them.

You also use commas to separate words in a list. They often replace *and* in this situation:

> He was a short, dark, grumpy, messy-haired teenage boy.

> She can speak first, second, or third in the debating team.

If you've got *and* in the list, it cancels out the need for a comma. 'The Australian flag is red, white and blue' needs just one comma.

Commas are great confusion-busters, as we already saw when we accidentally ate Grandad for dinner. Watch out for sentences like this, though, which are very common:

> I went with my mum, her sister and her business partner.

It's not clear from this whether there are three people or two. A comma will fix it.

Take care with commas

Commas only belong between ideas that are connected. If you put one between two ideas that are disconnected and don't relate, it's called a 'run-on sentence'. It will not impress markers. 'I'm sorry I'm late, the bus never came' should really be two short, separate sentences. If you're using a LOT of commas, you might be overdoing it. Think about replacing some with other punctuation, or using a full stop and starting a new sentence.

 NERD'S CORNER

How many commas can one list take?

You can stare down your nose and feel superior once you know about this.

In Australia we usually put just one comma in a three-item list, before the *and*: 'For breakfast I eat oranges, pears and apples'. But hop on a plane to the USA and you will be expected to use two commas: 'For breakfast I eat oranges, pears, and apples'.

It's mostly up to you to decide whether to use it, but sometimes it's essential to make your meaning clear.

Suppose you write 'I'd like to thank my parents, the coach and the Principal'. Are you the child of the coach and the Principal? If not, you need to write 'I'd like to thank my parents, the coach, and the Principal'. That extra comma makes all the difference.

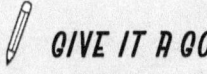
GIVE IT A GO

Here's some practice for you. Think about where commas should go in the following sentences, and notice the way their location completely changes the meaning.

> Before moving the guests my cousin and aunts rolled up the rugs.

It's ambiguous. Who was moving? And who helped roll up the rugs? Commas required!

> Before moving, the guests, my cousins and aunts helped roll up the rugs.

Now you can see that everyone was moving and everyone helped roll up the rugs. It would be completely different if you wrote:

> Before moving the guests, my cousins and aunts helped roll up the rugs.

Here the guests are being moved, after the cousins and aunts rolled up the rugs. Different punctuation, different meanings.

- **Semicolons** are the next weight up in pauses. You need a semicolon to put a break between two substantial, equally important and related parts of a sentence. They're often used between two sentence parts that each contain lists.

    > We've got ham, cheese, bread, tomatoes and lettuce; tomato sauce, mayonnaise and mustard.

    The first part of the sentence deals with the sandwiches, the second part with the sauces.

    You can also use a semicolon to split up two equally important parts of the same sentence:

    > Suddenly she found herself in a darkened room with no windows; she could not see the way forward or the way back.

    It's tricky to use semicolons properly. They are complex and we don't need them very often. They are rarely essential, but impressive when used properly.

- **Colons** share part of the same name, but are quite different from a semicolon. You use one before beginning a list.

    > We needed four things to go camping: a tent, a sleeping bag, a groundsheet and fine weather.

You also need it when you are giving an example or explaining a general statement you've just made.

> I achieved my life's ambition: winning an argument with my brother.

Wait a sec!

There are three forms of punctuation that let you block and unblock the flow of ideas, without ending the sentence.

- **Brackets** put a 'fence' around something that interrupts the rest of the sentence. What's inside the brackets is an aside – not the main idea. Usually you need them for giving additional information or explaining something. Quite often commas or dashes will work just as well.

  > My school (the newest in the area) is doing well in sports.

  > Our dog (a Jack Russell) likes chasing birds.

  If your brackets are at the end of a sentence, you need to figure out where to put the full stop. If the brackets don't contain a full sentence, the full stop goes outside them. If it IS a full sentence, the full stop goes *inside* them.

Try our usual test: remove the brackets and their contents, punctuate the sentence correctly, then drop the bracketed bit back in.

I love rockclimbing (my brother doesn't).

I love rockclimbing. (My brother likes surfing.)

- **Dashes** do nearly the same job as commas or brackets. They create a pause and allow you to insert an extra idea into your sentence. The examples of brackets above would be just as good with dashes instead.

  Our dog – a Jack Russell – likes chasing birds.

But you don't want to use too many, because they sound breathless and hectic when a lot of them are used close together.

  Our dog – a Jack Russell – chases birds all the time – like a rocket – off out of the park – before we even see her go.

- **Ellipsis** is a fancy name (from Greek) for those three dots that indicate that something is missing (…). You might have deliberately left some words out of a quote to shorten it. The ellipsis shows where you've done this:

  Australians all … are young and free

 **WARNING!**

Dashes and hyphens

It's easy to confuse a dash with a **hyphen**. A dash is longer than a hyphen and is a different character on your keyboard. The hyphen also does a different job. It joins two words together to make them work as one.

Some people have hyphens in their names: 'Mary-Louise', 'Jean-Paul'.

Most hyphens make two words work as a single adjective: 'My long-term goal is to study medicine'.

A missing or misplaced hyphen is one of those grammar booby traps you don't want to fall into. 'Ten-week-old chickens' are birds that are ten weeks old. That's not the same as 'Ten week-old chickens', which are ten baby birds.

Make sure you're saying what you mean!

The ellipsis is also used to imply words that don't need to be stated:

If he doesn't get it right this time …

And, of course, there are those wobbly grey dots, also called ellipsis, that tell you someone is typing when you are having a text conversation with them.

Speech and quotes

Speech marks, also called **inverted commas** or **quotation marks**, are for when you're using someone else's words, not your own. We use double quotes ("…") to show direct speech, and single quotes ('…') for quoting someone else's words.

You need to put one mark at the start, and another at the end, of what was said, like this:

> "I hate getting up early!" said Jordan.

> 'Four legs good. Two legs bad' is a slogan in the book *Animal Farm*.

Punctuating a quote within direct speech can be a challenge. It will look like this:

> Titus was saying "We have a test on Hamlet's 'To be or not to be' speech after lunch", when a parrot landed on his shoulder and said "That is the question"!

Where do they go?

The rule is if the punctuation is for what the person is saying, it goes inside the speech marks. If the punctuation relates to the sentence wrapped around what the person says, it goes outside.

"Are you going to the ball tonight?" asked Cinderella sadly.

"Yes," replied her sister, "but you're not."

"Well, I should certainly like to go," Cinderella replied. "Do you think it will be fun? My godmother says 'don't give up hope.'"

The Ugly Sister replied, "I wouldn't hold your breath."

"Ah, don't say that!"

Apostrophe

Oh dear, where do we start? The apostrophe is doomed. It is the most misused, misunderstood, unfairly treated member of the punctuation family. It has a terrible time, and it doesn't deserve it. It looks like a comma but it sits upstairs with the speech marks. It can do only two things.

It stands in when a letter has been taken out of a word to shorten it and make it easier to say. Easy everyday examples are *do not*, which becomes *don't*; or *will not*, which we've shortened to *won't*. You can see easily that you just remove some letters and replace them with an apostrophe instead. What could be simpler?

The second use for an apostrophe is to show possession. On page 64 we've talked about possessive pronouns: '*my* book', '*her* hat'. When we want to say that something owns something else, but without using pronouns, we need an apostrophe.

> The referee's whistle.
>
> Mum's towel.
>
> The cat's bowl.

Adding *'s* is all you need to do to show that something belongs to something else.

I just don't know what's difficult about that. It beats me why it should cause so much trouble, yet the apostrophe is the most tortured piece of punctuation in the English language.

The idea of *'s* has somehow got into people's heads as a general rule. So because we use the letter *s* to make a plural noun, people go ahead and add an apostrophe as well. Trust me, all the roadside fruit stalls in all the world advertising melon's and mango's and banana's are never going to make this right. An apostrophe has nothing to do with a plural. NOTHING. NOT EVER. NEVER.

Sadly, many people think the apostrophe is on the way out. Uncertainty about what's correct, abuse by signs in shops, and texters leaving them out in the rush to send their messages, all create enough confusion for people to say 'too hard' and not even try. For any student however, incorrect use will not be permitted. You have to get this one right.

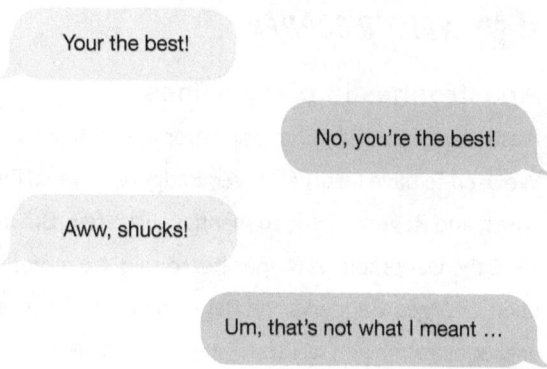

The mystery of the ss'

Troublespots lurk when you need an apostrophe, but the word it's working with already ends in an s, or – worse – a double s. It's easy enough when it's Tom's towel, but what if the towel belongs to Tess? This is one of those soft and bendy 'rules'. You can write *Tess's towel*, and double the *s*; but some people would write *Tess' towel*. *The class's behaviour* looks weird but it's correct. If the noun is a plural, so it's already ending in *s*, you normally put the apostrophe after it: *A girls' school; the players' equipment.*

 **NERD'S CORNER**

Apostrophes in place names

Australian places don't have apostrophes in their names. We used to have George's River, Badgery's Creek, French's Forest and Regent's Park, to mention just a few. But in 1966 the Geographical Names Board said 'No more!' It's been Georges, Badgerys and Regents ever since. The only apostrophe you will see in a place name is a case like O'Donnell – though I reckon they'll be whiting that out before too long as well.

4
SENTENCES

A sentence is group of words that begins with a capital letter and ends with a full stop, right?

Yes. But it might be better to think of it as a combination of words which all work together to tell us something.

Individual words aren't much use on their own. When they are connected up into a longer chain that creates meaning, that's different. *That's* what we call a sentence. We create even longer chains by combining sentences into paragraphs, stories, essays, novels and so on. But the sentence is the fundamental building block for the English language.

When speaking, we get away with using sentences that are just bits, or fragments. We don't even bother to complete our sentences some of the time.

'Coffee?' 'Sure.' 'Where?' 'Don't mind, your turn.'

There's no verb there, but so long as the person we're speaking to can follow, it's OK. In writing, however, that is not OK.

A grammarian will tell you that a sentence is a group of words that has meaning and contains a verb. The fact that it has a verb is most important. If it doesn't, it can't be a sentence.

To become a sentence-buster you'll need some definitions.

Terminology time

Phrase or fragment	A group of words that makes sense but has no verb
Clause	A group of words that has a verb and makes sense
Finite verb	A verb that has a subject
Transitive verb	A verb that has an object
Subject	The doer of the action in a sentence or clause
Object	The person or thing on the receiving end of the action
Simple sentence	One verb, one subject, one (optional) object
Compound sentence	Two verbs in one sentence
Complex sentence	More than two verbs in a sentence
Noun, verb, adjectival OR adverbial phrases or clauses	A group of words acting as a single part of speech
Syntax	The order of words and phrases

Four sentence types

There must be three types of sentences because when we looked at punctuation on page 111 we learned that there are three ways to end a sentence.

Sentences

Fooled you! In fact, there are *four* types of sentences.

1. The first one is a simple statement. It can be called a **declarative sentence**, but **statement** is a perfectly good description. In any case, it gets a full stop.
2. A **question** is also a type of sentence. End it with a question mark. Its fancy label is **interrogative**.
3. An **exclamation** (no points for guessing how to end that sentence!) comes next.
4. The fourth is a **command**, also called an **imperative**: 'Sit down!', 'Over here!', 'Pay attention!', 'Shut up!'

NERD'S CORNER

'Understood'

'So', I hear you asking, 'if a verb is necessary to make a sentence, how come there isn't one in the command "Over here!"'? Great question. In English, we take short cuts, and sometimes the verb (and other parts of speech) are not openly expressed, but we still know what's meant. We say the missing words are 'understood' or implied. We're really saying '[You, please come] over here!', '[You, please] sit down!

Three sentence patterns

1. **Simple** sentences have just one verb.
2. **Compound** sentences have two verbs.
3. **Complex** sentences have more than two verbs.

Simple sentences

It's possible to have a sentence that is just a subject and a verb.

'I will' is an example of this – handy for anyone getting married.

More often, however, the simplest sentences are just subject-verb-object.

I owe $10. — Subject / Verb / Object

You dropped the ball!

She loves me.

I passed the exam?

My dog likes bones.

A sentence like this is stripped right down to its bones. It's direct and can be very striking, as the boxer Muhammad ('I am the greatest!') Ali knew.

Very few sentences, however, are this simple. A 'one verber' is clear enough, but it's basic. To add interest and extend what you say, you want more depth and detail.

Compound sentences

If there are two verbs in a sentence we say it's a **compound** sentence.

> The little girl gave a cry of amazement and looked about her.

Complex sentences

Complex sentences have *more* than two verbs – underlined here.

> 'It is kind of you to wear that,' said Boq, 'because blue is the color of the Munchkins, and white is the witch color, so we know you are a friendly witch'.

Getting inside a sentence

Wrapped around these verbs, and helping to make the sentences longer, are additional chains of words called **phrases** and **clauses**. Verbs, clauses and phrases are a bit like the threads in a fabric. They are woven together to create a sentence. The arrangement of the 'threads' produces different results.

Phrases

Phrases (also called **fragments**) are groups of words that aren't sentences, do make sense, but have no verb.

> here at school
>
> long brown hair
>
> high-heeled shoes
>
> early one morning

They can be added to any sentence, but they can't live alone. We need the surrounding context to get their meaning. Let's use a few phrases to jazz some simple sentences up.

> She loves me **truly, madly, deeply**.
>
> My dog likes **nice juicy** bones **for a treat**.
>
> I passed the **horrendously difficult almost impossible** exam **with full marks**.

(handwritten annotation: Phrases)

A phrase can do the work of a noun, an adjective, an adverb or a preposition. It would be good if you could recognise these.

- Noun phrases: *my brother's bike, top grade tennis, world-famous rock star.*

- Adjectival phrases: *golden haired, rickety old, light coloured.*
- Prepositional phrases: *over the moon, beside the river.*
- Adverbial phrases: these help us know when (time), where (place), why (reason), and how (manner). Here's an example:

> Late last night (time), in the heart of the forest (place), wanting to escape (reason), without being noticed (manner), I (subject) silently slipped away (verb phrase).

Writing well with phrases

Phrases embellish your sentences and provide the details a reader needs to be interested.

Let me mess around with Lewis Carroll's writing once again.

> Suddenly she came upon a table with a key on it, and Alice's first thought was that it might belong to one of the doors but, alas! either the locks were too large, or the key was too small, for it would not open any of them.

Not bad. But here is what he actually wrote. See how the phrases (underlined) make it live.

> Suddenly she came upon <u>a little three-legged table</u>, all made <u>of solid glass</u>; there was <u>nothing on it</u> except <u>a tiny golden key</u>, and Alice's <u>first thought</u> was that it might belong to <u>one of the doors of the hall</u>; but, alas! either the locks were too large, or the key was too small, but <u>at any rate</u> it would not open any of them.

Clauses

To use more verbs in a sentence, you are going to need clauses. When I explain a clause you're going to say 'that's just like a sentence!', and it is. Here we go anyway. A clause is a group of words that makes sense and contains a verb.

Clause types

Clauses come in two varieties: **independent** and **dependent**.

An **independent** clause stands alone and can look after itself. It's good enough to be a complete sentence. If it contains the most important information in the sentence it's called the **principal clause**, just like the Principal of a school.

A **dependent clause** ties itself to another clause. It's a parasite, it needs to be in a symbiotic relationship, it can't exist alone. These 'helping' clauses are sometimes called **subordinate** clauses. Subordinate means 'under', so the name shows there's an up / down connection. They're supporting another clause.

In this passage, the independent clauses are in italics, and the dependent clauses are underlined.

> Suddenly *she came upon a little three-legged table*, <u>all made of solid glass</u>; *there was nothing on it except a tiny golden key*, and *Alice's first thought was that it might belong to one of the doors of the hall*; but, alas! <u>either the locks were too large</u>, <u>or the key was too small</u>, but at any rate *it would not open any of them*.

Go to page 85 for a list of joining words that you can use to connect clauses.

Writing well with clauses

Without clauses, every sentence would follow the same format: subject, verb and object. Most sentences would be short and choppy, like this:

> I teach English. I work in a high school. I enjoy it.
> The students are nice. They work hard. I like them.

If we change a few sentences into phrases, lose some verbs and connect it all up with conjunctions and pronouns, we get something like this:

> I *enjoy* teaching <u>high school English</u>, because I *like* my <u>nice hard-working students</u>.

There are two verbs, *enjoy* and *like*, and two noun phrases (underlined). There's also a principal clause ('I enjoy teaching high school English') and an adverbial clause of reason ('because I like my nice hard-working students').

It flows better. By connecting everything into one sentence, we end up with a unified sense of what I want to say.

How to write better sentences

Here are some boredom-busters to liven up your prose.

1 Delay the principal clause

It's like telling a joke. Hold the punchline back; add some other clauses first, and delay the main action. Deliver the principal clause late, or last.

Let's remix a sentence we looked at earlier.

> Late last night, in the heart of the forest, wanting to escape without being noticed, I silently slipped away.

The principal clause is last. All those other phrases and clauses just wind you up. You have to know what's going on; you can't stop till you know what happened, so you have to keep on reading.

More options:

> I silently slipped away in the heart of the forest late last night, wanting to escape without being noticed.

> In the heart of the forest late last night, wanting to escape, I silently slipped away without being noticed.

> Wanting to escape without being noticed, I silently slipped away late last night in the heart of the forest.

Which of the three rewrites do you like best? Why?

2 Use unusual clause and phrase positions

Remember that clauses and phrases can do the work of a single part of speech. Try splicing them into your sentences for variety. Use:

An adjectival clause (begins with *who*, *which* or *that*).

> That trapeze artist <u>who floats like an angel</u> is performing next Tuesday.

An adverbial clause. These tell us where, when, how or why. (They start with *since, until, while, as soon as, because, although, while, though, unless, in case*.)

> <u>Although he stole the playlunches</u>, Balthazar was not a criminal.

A noun clause (often starts with *that*, *what* or *whatever*).

> <u>Whatever I do</u>, I still fall over.

To build tension and hook the reader, try using:
A noun phrase as a subject:

> <u>A black shadow</u> dropped down into the circle.

A noun phrase as an object:

> They saw Bagheera, <u>the Black Panther</u>.

An adjectival phrase to start a sentence:

> <u>Silent and terrified</u>, the animals crept back into the barn …

A string of different clauses and phrases, to build up layers of detail, like this example from *Animal Farm*, to build up layers of detail.

> At one end of the big barn, on a sort of raised platform, Major was already ensconced on his bed of straw, under a lantern which hung from a beam.

3   Add rhetorical devices

Repetition

Run Toto, run!

Triads

There were <u>more</u> songs, <u>more</u> speeches, <u>more</u> processions.

Muriel was <u>dead</u>; Bluebell, Jessie, and Pincher were <u>dead</u>. Jones too was <u>dead</u>.

Contrasts

… either the locks were too large, or the key was too small …

4   Start each sentence differently

Use a mix of **where** and **when** words – *under, over, beside, behind, near, through*:

At the gate they paused …

Use prepositions – *before, after, during*:

After his hoof had healed up, Boxer worked harder than ever.

Use days of the week, months of the year, times of day, seasons:

> One Sunday morning, when the animals assembled …
>
> November came, with raging south-west winds.
>
> Late one evening in the summer, a sudden rumour ran round.
>
> By the autumn the animals were tired but happy.
>
> Suddenly, early in the spring, an alarming thing was discovered.

Sentence diagramming

I want to introduce you to an old-fashioned but fun teaching tool. It's called sentence diagramming. It was taught in American schools when your grandparents were children. Once you know your parts of speech, and how to pick out subjects, complements and objects, you can create a visual map of how sentence parts all click together.

You begin by marking the division between verb and subject, and then insert the modifiers and other parts of speech in other, designated places.

You're going to wind up with something like this:

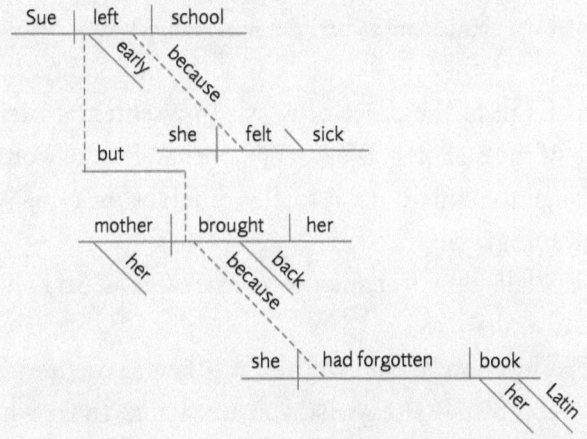

If you're the kind of person who likes drawing, and if you think in terms of structures and patterns, you are going to love it. Google it for detailed instructions.

5
SYNTAX: GET YOUR WORDS IN ORDER

This has nothing to do with sin or taxes (which would be an odd combination).

> I was waiting for the bus when suddenly it hit me: my sentences are sometimes misleading.

In English, the order of words in a sentence carries much of the meaning. We can take the same set of words, rearrange them, and get a totally different meaning, or no meaning at all.

'Australia beat Sri Lanka' is not the same as 'Sri Lanka beat Australia'.

The location of the two nouns – before or after the verb – completely alters what you are saying. To say what you mean, those positions have to be right. Otherwise someone will win more games than they should.

That's not the only case where word order matters. Here are a few more examples:

Syntax: get your words in order

If I ask 'Did you get your beach towel dry?', it is not the same as asking 'Did you get your dry beach towel?'

In the first case, the word *dry* is part of a verb (to *get dry*). In the second example, it's an adjective modifying the noun *beach towel*. But it's only the word order which tells us that.

Limiting words, like *almost, hardly, nearly, just* and *only*, are danger zones. Shift them into a new place and your meaning shifts too.

> Santa visited *only* us.
>
> Santa *only* visited us.
>
> *Only* Santa visited us.

Or what about this:

> I *almost* want nothing.
>
> I want *almost* nothing.

Sometimes, though (this is English after all), you can change the order around without changing the meaning. 'I saw him a minute ago' and 'A minute ago I saw him', mean the same thing. It would not, however, make sense to say 'I saw a minute ago him'.

Syntax includes not only vocabulary and word order, but also the accurate use of punctuation and pronouns. All together they will get your meaning across. If you're not mastering syntax, you might say something you did not mean to say, or say something so confusing the reader does not know what you meant to say.

 **FUN STUFF**

Poor syntax can be a sign of fuzzy thinking, careless writing or weak language skills. Here are two real-life signs:

SUCCESSFUL MEN'S SPA

I think this sign is telling me it's a spa for successful men. Or maybe a successful spa for men? I am not sure what the owner really wanted to say. It needs a rewrite.

> In loving memory of
> Jane Roe
> Who never saw a dog and didn't smile

This is a tribute to a warm-hearted lady who loved dogs. Sadly, poor syntax means it can be interpreted as meaning quite the opposite to what was intended.

Syntax: get your words in order

 NERD'S CORNER

Yoda-speak

Q: Why such weird way Yoda speaks?

A: Yoda uses a kind of syntax that is not much like English, but is still understandable. He uses weird word order to sound ancient and wise.

Q: Why does weird word order make him sound ancient and wise?

A: Because Shakespeare did it. The weirdness is because the normal subject-verb-object sentence pattern is tipped up and twisted. It's called inversion. Here are a few Shakespearean examples of the same thing:

> What light through yonder window breaks? (*Romeo and Juliet*)
>
> Saw you him today? (*Romeo and Juliet*)
>
> Rude am I in speech (*Othello*)
>
> Round about the cauldron go (*Macbeth*)

Shakespeare did it for poetic effect, but he wasn't the only one turning his subject-verb-object patterns around. It was done in much earlier poetry, and The King James Version of the Bible (1611), which was widely used for nearly 400 years, had many of these inversions in its wonderful verses.

Continued...

Part 2: Essential skills for writing well

> *Yoda-speak continued...*
>
> Make straight in the desert a highway [Isaiah 40:3]
>
> All we like sheep have gone astray, we have turned every one to his own way [Isaiah 53:6]
>
> So, for hundreds of years and many generations, people have been familiar with this 'flipping' technique. Yoda-speak is the *Star Wars* screen writers' way of suggesting his ancient Jedi heritage.
>
> Maybe you too can upsell yourself and gain status by talking like Yoda does. Next time someone asks what you want to do when you finish school, say 'A computer scientist will I be'. Or tell your parents that 'For Christmas a bike would I like'; or end an argument by saying 'Speak to you again I will not'.

6
TONE: REACHING YOUR AUDIENCE

Tone is the way you speak to, or about, someone or something. It's just like your tone of voice. If you've been rude to a teacher they might say 'I don't like your tone'. If you deliver a vote of thanks and sound sincere and convincing, someone might say you got 'just the right tone'.

Tone is an important creative choice. It's a bit like deciding what to wear. How do you want to come across? It has to be suitable for the audience, purpose and context, but you also want to make a certain impression. It's a matter of style.

When you write, you can adopt a neutral tone, or a humorous, wry or serious tone. Maybe you could choose a friendly, warm, gentle and kind tone. Perhaps you need to sound academic, authoritative, like you really know your stuff. Check the information on **register** on pages 160–165 to see some of the options. There are lots more.

The style of language you use has to cut through and work with your readers. You need to choose your words purposefully. People need to be able to follow your ideas and get the message you want. You must be certain that the words you choose will do that job.

> **WARNING!**
>
> **Formality rules**
>
> It's a big mistake by student writers not to make the tone formal enough. In any assessment you should imagine you are writing for the Principal, or your scary aunt, the one who hates kids and never smiles.

7
PARAGRAPHS

No matter what you're writing, you need to divide it into paragraphs. A paragraph is a chunk of text that's all about one idea. It will be at least several sentences long. If it's more than half a page, you've probably gone too far.

Some young writers have the idea that paragraphing is an option. It isn't. You will always be penalised if your text is not properly divided up.

Perfect paragraphs

If you leave everything piling up in one long piece of writing, it soon becomes exhausting and confusing for your reader. Just look at a whole page of unbroken text. Even thinking about reading it wears me out.

However, a page that's broken into several paragraphs (like this one) looks well organised and orderly, don't you think? At a glance you can see you'll be able to move through it comfortably.

A single idea

A paragraph has to be about just **one** thing. We're looking for **unity**. A paragraph doesn't wander. It is sharp, focused, self-contained and on point. When someone is reading your work they're going to pick up its one main idea.

A nice, strong central idea holds the paragraph up, like the trunk of a tree. The branches and leaves of the tree are the sentences inside the paragraph, which tell the story or explain your meaning.

How do you do it? Easy. When you open a new idea or sub-topic, you need to start a new paragraph. Any time you begin a new thought or issue, or there's a change in time or place, that tells you it's new paragraph time.

We put a break between paragraphs on the page, to show the break between the different ideas that are in each one. If you're using a computer, you use a two-line space. If you're handwriting, you start a new line, then indent, which means leaving a centimetre between the left-hand edge of the page and where you start writing.

Logical flow

When you're inside the paragraph, those sentences have to follow each other in a sensible way. Sentences need to be complete, and the reader needs to feel a connection from one sentence to another.

Paragraphs

All your thoughts have to be connected up. That's why we need conjunctions, prepositions, pronouns, different types of clauses and all of the other features that we've been learning about. These all stitch your ideas together so that instead of being separate, disjointed little piles of thoughts, they're connected into a nice coherent whole.

The trouble is that young writers often don't notice when one idea stops and another idea starts. It's your overheated and feverish minds: they race so fast, you just can't stop them. But stop you must. It's important to get used to finding the resting place, where one idea is done with, and you're moving on to a new one. That's the time to start a new paragraph.

Separate but related

Every paragraph has a different job to do.

- The opening paragraph will always introduce the topic, and tell the reader what's going on.
- The paragraphs that follow each develop the topic more.
- Finally, there will be a paragraph which closes everything down and concludes it.

Each paragraph is unique. They are like siblings, all part of one family, but one paragraph should not be too much like another. It's important to make them different, while they still fit together, like separate but related parts.

Variety and balance

To create variety, you must start each paragraph in a different way. And it's not only your starting sentences that should be varied; the sentences within the paragraphs should be varied as well. Use different lengths and different word patterns.

Here are four sentences that open the first four paragraphs in Chapter 2 of *The Wonderful Wizard of Oz*.

> She was awakened by a shock, so sudden and severe that if Dorothy had not been lying on the soft bed she might have been hurt …

> The cyclone had set the house down very gently – for a cyclone – in the midst of a country of marvelous beauty …

> While she stood looking eagerly at the strange and beautiful sights, she noticed coming toward her a group of the queerest people she had ever seen …

> Three were men and one a woman, and all were oddly dressed.

For a start, just look at their first words. See how much variety there is already?

Then look at sentence length. The first three are quite long. They flow along with multiple clauses and phrases to pad them out, but the fourth sentence is short and simple. It makes an important point in very few words.

The first sentence uses the passive voice, but the second sentence is active voice and puts the cyclone back in charge. The third sentence is a great example of delaying the principal clause till the end. (See page 134 for more about this.)

Altogether, sentence variety is a good way to make your writing interesting.

{ PART 3 }

HOW TO BE A GOOD WRITER

The only way you can be a writer is with language. A musician has melody, harmony, tempo, rhythm, different keys and different instruments that can all be used for different moods and effects; a painter has colour and a choice of paint types; but a writer just has words.

It's the way a writer uses words that makes the writing vivid, involving and gripping; or emotional, tender and heartwarming; or entertaining, amusing and funny; or informative, clear and precise.

WRITING IS A PROCESS

Nobody sits down and tosses a great piece of writing off first try. Writing well takes time.

There are five steps in the writing process. Depending how much time you have and how long the piece is, they could take anything from half an hour to weeks, or even months to complete.

The five steps are:

1 planning
2 drafting / writing
3 resting
4 editing
5 rewriting.

Steps 4 and 5 are repeated for as long as it takes to be happy with the result.

Steps 1 and 2 are hard work. We'll look at them more closely in the sections on Creative, Persuasive and Analytical Writing in Part 4 of the book.

The best part about writing is step 3. You should never hand in anything you've written unless you've revised it. The best thing you can do for your prose is to LEAVE IT ALONE. Let it sit. Look at it again in a few days time. While you're resting it will settle and sort itself out in your mind. Next time you look at what you wrote you will see the lack of clarity, the confusion, the not-very-tidy parts. You will then fix them up.

1
PLANNING

Purpose, audience, context

These are the golden triangle of good writing. Go get a felt-tip pen and write them on the bathroom mirror. Every time you look at yourself you will be reminded of their saintly status, their high power. The fact that they reign over all you write.

The reason these three are so important is that everything you write, and everything you read and then write about, needs to take them into account.

To write well means being clear about these three things, and fitting what you say and how you say it around them. You must be sure about:

1 what you want to do (purpose)
2 who it's for (audience), and
3 the situation surrounding it (context).

The principle is that you need to adjust your language to do the best job for the purpose, in the situation you are writing for, and get through to your readers – your audience.

Here's a hypothetical. Is it a good idea to submit an exam paper with love hearts drawn on it? Or funny faces? Or to write with lots of capital letters, underlining and exclamation marks? Or how about using lots of playground slang? Foooolish ...! These are not appropriate ways to write, in that situation.

Think about the golden triangle.

- Your **purpose** is to demonstrate your skills in the subject and earn marks.
- Your **audience** is whoever will be marking your work.
- The **context** is a formal, structured one – it's an exam, an assessment.

You need to show you take this seriously. Use a language style that sits well with that.

Let's switch to a new situation. You are writing a birthday card for your best friend. Now everything's changed. Love hearts and lots of enthusiastic exclamation marks might be perfect. They are informal, they show your strength of feeling. They work in this context, because the audience is a friend, and your purpose is to celebrate and feel good.

We need to look a bit harder at all this.

Purpose

You need to know where you want to end up. Sound simple? It might, but it's not. There could be lots of options. It isn't enough to have the goal 'write a good essay' or 'write a great advertisement'. State your purpose in some detail. For example, 'my purpose is to show my teacher that I understand the main character in the novel we've studied'. Or 'my purpose is to sell tickets to the school play'.

Try always to answer these questions:

- Why are you doing this? What is the aim?
- What should the reader remember after you've finished?
- What type of language skills do you need to show?

Think about some of the things you've read recently. If it's a sport report, or a fashion blog, or a movie review, it might be pretty easy to grasp the author's purpose, as well as the audience it's written for, and the context.

But what about more literary writing? What is a poet on about? Have you ever considered an author's purpose in writing fiction? You need to be able to see the purpose in others' writing as well as being clear about your own.

Context and Audience

An author's purpose very often arises from the context. A poet might intend to stir emotions and provoke thought because of something that has happened to them. A novel or play might make us stop and contemplate something that is common to human experience. It may be written in praise or sorrow, or to be critical, or build understanding. It might just be to entertain us, to make us laugh.

The *form* the writer uses makes a vital difference to how these ideas come across.

If you've read novels like *To Kill A Mockingbird* by Harper Lee, or *Animal Farm* by George Orwell, you know that they intend to be critical, and give a warning about troublesome flaws in society. So does *The Hunger Games* by Suzanne Collins. These are stories whose context – the state of the world at the time they were written – is the reason they were written in the first place.

George Orwell was concerned about the dangers of dictatorship. *Animal Farm* is an allegorical fable, a short, childlike tale whose simplicity makes its brutality all the more shocking. Harper Lee shows us the clash of social and moral values surrounding race relations in the United States. *To Kill A Mockingbird* is told through the eyes of a seven-year-old, whose innocence sharpens the contrast between good and evil. Suzanne Collins' reality TV survival gameshow is a warning about the future of our airhead, entertainment-soaked world. *The Hunger*

Games is dystopian fiction, a wildly popular genre with its intended audience of young adults.

Language 'registers'

When you write an essay or a creative piece, your language must be suitable for the genre and the person who will read it.

Most of our conversation is casual. We don't need it to be polished. We usually speak with people we know, about things we are familiar with. It's all quite easy, and comfortable. We often use vague words rather than being specific. In fact, if you read transcriptions of what's actually been said by someone – even professional speakers like broadcasters – you will be amazed at how confused it sounds, but listeners make allowances for this and can still understand.

We also make changes to the way we speak depending on the situation we're in, who we're talking to, and what it's about. We don't do it consciously. The change seems to happen by itself, as if we have an internal channel changer that resets automatically and tunes us to the right mode.

Unfortunately none of that is true for writing. Writing takes thought and effort, in order to say exactly what we mean. One part of this is using the right register.

Take a look at this thermometer. It's a kind of formality measure. At the top is formal structured language, used when people are distant with each other. At the bottom we have intimate language, used by people who are close and know each other well. In between these two points there are other 'grades' of formality. These are known as **language registers**. If you are talking to the Prime Minister, or applying for a scholarship or a job, the right register won't be the same one you use for family and close friends.

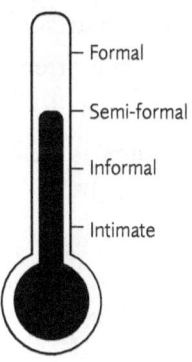

To use the wrong register is an error. You will sound awkward and inappropriate, or possibly even rude. It's just not acceptable to speak to a policeman in the same way you'd speak to your baby brother, or to email your teacher using the language you'd use in the playground with your friends.

Intimate language

This is private. It's the way you communicate with family, very close friends, boyfriend and girlfriend, husband and wife, parents to children. There are not many boundaries; you say what you think.

Characteristics: Intimate language has its own set of words and phrases, pet names, nicknames and code words that only apply to this context. It's used at home, away from the public eye. Keep it there! Using intimate language in a non-intimate situation might give offence.

Real-life uses: The written form is usually on social media, or in texts or emails. There might be graphics and emojis, and photos as well as words. Here's a mum emailing when she's mad:

> Unbelievable – please don't tell me you really did this? We will have words!

Informal, conversational language

This is the language used between friends. It has a familiar, easy-going tone. It can include slang and colloquialisms.

Characteristics: Informal language is easy to read and understand. It uses common words and sentence patterns to create a friendly connection between writer and reader. Your vocabulary and sentences can mirror the way you speak.

Real-life uses: The written form is used every day in emails or text messages, and is also the language we see often online, and in some books.

> Hey! I have been having the hardest time picking outfits. So I almost literally jumped OVER the moon when I found this A-MA-ZING jacket.

Semi-formal language

This is a notch or two up, a bit more formal. Think of the way a teacher would write to your parents, or you would write to your Principal, or to some other expert, like a doctor or a professor; a person you know in an official rather than a personal way.

Characteristics: You address them using their title (Mr, Ms, Dr), not their first name. Your language is polite and respectful, and focused solely on the issue at hand. You use complete, properly written sentences. You can sound friendly, but do not use slang or make jokes, or say anything that undermines the professional context. If you are asking for something, include all the necessary information (and no more!) and the reasons you'd like their assistance.

Real-life uses: Communicating with teachers, lecturers or others you have only a professional connection with. Asking for, or providing assistance, seeking information, inviting them to attend something, seeking clarification of something, asking a favour (for example, an extension on an assignment). Here are some email examples; see what you think of them.

> hi – send me the notes for today's class
>
> Hello I was sick today. What did I miss?

I hope that you can see that this is NOT the way to speak to someone who teaches you. No greeting, no signoff, no gratitude. These writers show no manners or respect. They're unlikely to get the help they want.

This is better:

> Dear Mr Feeltheburn,
>
> I have just checked the team lists and found my name in two places. Could you please tell where I am supposed to be.
>
> Yours sincerely
> Mack, Year 9

Formal language

This is 'proper'. It is careful and well thought out. It is a kind of public performance, and it's often one-way communication, because a response is not necessarily expected.

Characteristics: You need complete sentences and an impersonal, non-emotional tone. It should sound reasonable, objective and serious. You may use the third person, and the passive voice. You might use technical terms. You should not be too conversational. What you write must be complete, and provide all relevant information in a concise form. Don't go into unnecessary detail.

Real-life uses: This is how academic essays and university, scholarship and job applications should be written. You also use this register if you have to provide a statement to the police, a court, or to an insurance company (if you have been involved in an accident for example). It's also the right register for opening a conversation with someone who is your superior, such as a teacher.

As a sample, here is a doctor, asking the authorities to help his patient at an upcoming exam. Note the formal tone and the way all the necessary information is included.

> To whom it may concern,
>
> Letitia Deletia is a Year 6 student who suffered a broken arm as a result of falling off her bike on February 28th. As she is sitting the Selective High School Placement test on March 15th, I request that the High Performing Students Unit provide her with assistance.
>
> She was certified by me at the Big Hospital Emergency Department as being unable to attend school for two weeks. She will be able to return to school on March 14th with limited capacity: unable to hold a pen or marker, unable to type, unable to lift or carry books, a laptop and other resources, due to her cast and splint.
>
> Signed
> Dr Verygood Bonefixer

Part 3: How to be a good writer

What not to do

Here is an exchange of emails where several registers are mixed up.

Dear Adalbert,

Apologies if I have misplaced something but I have no record of receiving your essay. Please get it in by tomorrow.

Sincerely,
Ms Flizzlewook

Semi-formal, Courteous.

I handed mine in to you on Friday it might not have been named but it was in inky black pen.

No greetings, no sign-off. Too informal.

Dear Adalbert,

I can't find an unnamed in inky black pen essay. Please submit by tomorrow, or take a detention.

Sincerely,
Ms Flizzlewook

Semi-formal. Still courteous.

It was handwritten.

No greeting or sign-off. Sounds rude.

You need to resubmit it Adalbert.

No greeting or sign-off. Sounds annoyed.

Misrepresentation – trying to sound friendly.

Miss, as we established earlier mine was handed in via a sheet paper which seems to have been

Planning

misplaced, having already done the work I thought it rather unfair to remember and resubmit the task. Further, I have had training Wednesday afternoon, Thursday morning and afternoon and maths exam tomorrow, these activities have created an extensive strain for time, in which I was unable to Resubmit the already completed task. I hope detention will no longer be necessary given the explanation, context and notice.

Passive voice: doesn't say 'you lost it'.

Overly long, too much information.

Regards,
Adalbert

Attempting to sound formal.

Sign off.

Now attempting to use proper formality.

Adalbert,

Your two-hour detention, issued by Ms Flizzlewook, for failure to submit an assignment, is on Tuesday 8 May. Please report to room 93 at 3.30pm. Failure to do so will result in a second detention. Sport training and exam preparation do not take priority over assessment tasks or detention.

Regards,
Mrs Flintface
Detentions manager

Formal, institutional communication.

Dear Ms Fizzelwook,

I write to advise that Adalbert Dwookman has withdrawn from your course.

Sincerely yours,
Foster Goodwork
Academic administrator

Formal, institutional.

2
DRAFTING AND WRITING

Structure

The exact way you organise your material depends on what format and text type you're writing. No matter what you write though, it's going to need a beginning, a middle and an end. That sounds very obvious. However, what exactly goes into the beginning, the middle and the end can vary greatly.

We have separate sections later in the book on persuasive, creative and analytical writing. In those pages you will be able to see some examples of how to structure your work. Let's just say for now that it's important to decide at the beginning what structure you're going to use.

Introductions – you need one

Imagine you just walked into a completely strange place, a plain building with no name on the front, no signage, and other ways to find out what it's for. Inside the building are some people, but though they're talking on phones and to each other, some are behind glass, and you don't quite hear what they say. There are also a few rows of seats. How do you feel? Confused? Hesitant? Cautious?

That feeling of confusion and uncertainty is exactly what it's like for a reader at the start of any piece of writing. A reader is disoriented, clueless about what will come next. This is a new place; they haven't been here before.

Now imagine that outside a helpful sign says 'Clinic', and some signs inside say 'Waiting area', 'Vaccinations this way', 'Emergency Department' and so on. Maybe there's a desk with a person sitting at it who asks what you've come in for and tells you where to go. Would you feel a bit less confused? A bit more confident about heading on in? Of course you would. That's because the signs and the greeter give your brain the information it needs to process and prepare for a visit to this place. Without them, you'd use a lot of brain power looking for clues to solve the problem of what this place is, before you get down to the business of getting medical attention.

In the same way that the person at the desk introduces you to the clinic, the start of a written piece must help the reader to know what they're about to get into.

In any piece of writing, you must orient the reader. The writer's first job is to help that reader find a way in. This is the job of the **Introduction**. It's important that your opening words arouse interest and create a connection so the reader knows the 'who, what, when, where, why' of what's coming up.

> 'Christmas won't be Christmas without any presents,' grumbled Jo, lying on the rug.
>
> 'It's so dreadful to be poor!' sighed Meg, looking down at her old dress.

That's the opening of *Little Women* by Louisa May Alcott. Straight away we know what's going on. I wrote 'How To Use This Book' on page 10. That's my introduction for you. And take a look at pages 216–217 for the openings of some famous, classic books. They are fiction, so we are being taken to an imaginary world of imaginary people and imaginary events. See how they help the reader into the story.

And in conclusion …

A well-developed conclusion brings your writing gracefully to an end. It's not as easy as it sounds though. In a fiction piece you might be tempted to say 'and then it was all over', or 'they went back to normal', or 'and then he woke up and discovered it was all a dream' or 'they lived happily ever after'. This is clichéd and you need to be more creative.

In a persuasive piece, you might end with a 'call to action' or a solution to the problem that you've been talking about. In an analytical piece of writing, you might restate your main idea and remind the readers of the steps you've just been through as you explored it. The trouble with this is it can be repetitive. A better idea might be to mention the most interesting or important things that you've written about. What message or information do you want readers to take away? Find a way of ending with a clear statement of your one big idea, so that it is really memorable. Or, even better, leave them with something to think about: 'It will be interesting to see how this develops', 'I wonder what further research may reveal'. Or, ask a question.

The writer's toolkit

Ideas

Writing needs to be about something. Well, 'duh'. It's known as OBI: One Big Idea. This gives your writing shape. Think of it as being like the route you take on a journey. There may be side streets and pathways that you detour down, but even with these diversions, you're always going somewhere; you have direction.

Figurative language

Writers use a range of word 'tricks' to help us understand their meaning. You should learn to use them too.

It's important also to recognise these techniques in other people's writing and be able to understand how they work. Why has the writer used THESE words? In English exams at school, you need to recognise a language technique and also explain the effect it produces.

Figurative language is not literally true. Sometimes known as **literary** or **language techniques**, figurative language relies on hidden meanings or word patterns for effect. It makes imaginative comparisons to help you see the world in new ways. It's a kind of 'special effects box'.

Some basic figurative techniques that you should have in your repertoire are:

- At the word and sentence level: alliteration, assonance, onomatopoeia, repetition, rhyme and rhythm, simile, metaphor, personification.
- At the paragraph or essay level: hyperbole, symbolism, imagery, tone.

But before we look at these, let me introduce you to the Number One figurative feature of all time.

Connotation

Some words are smugglers. They carry hidden meanings. We call this **connotation**, and it's the key to understanding how words and phrases suggest something without saying it openly.

Meaning operates on two levels: there's the dictionary definition, but words also have implied meanings that come, informally, from the way they are used. They gather extra meanings because of who uses them, and the situations they're used in.

The problem is that once a word loses its strict relationship to the dictionary meaning, and picks up those extra, suggested meanings, not everybody understands all words the same way.

If I describe something as 'cheap', you might think it doesn't cost a lot of money – which will be true. But in relation to what? How do we judge? If it's a cheap Coke, that sounds like I got it at a good price. But what if it's a cheap wedding dress? You might get the idea that it's not very good quality and that I don't think much of it. Did I say that? No, I did not. You could possibly interpret it the opposite way: that it's better because it's cheap, and I value it more. Did I say that? No, I did not.

'Cheap' may or may not be a good thing. I have no idea which one of those meanings you will 'get'. You just 'read between the lines' and drew your own conclusions.

For this reason, I may be misunderstood.

If someone says, 'Want to come over and eat?', you will expect a friendly meal at their house. You will likely come as you are, without going to any trouble to get dressed up, and everything will be relaxed.

However, if someone says, 'I'd like to invite you to dine with us tonight', you will get a rather different picture. Maybe you will imagine a tablecloth, wine glasses, flowers ... something formal where you need your best manners. In this case, you are likely to put on clean clothes, be sure to arrive on time, keep your feet off the furniture and say 'please' and 'thank you' often.

Without me saying anything at all about the way the room would be set up, or the atmosphere that will surround the dinner, just using the words *invite* and *dine* gave you those hints of what to expect.

Yes, here it is again – our old friend context. The connotations of words depend a lot on the situation they are used in.

Imagine I tell you that the weather is 'fine', or it's 'fine' for you to go to a party – you'll think I'm telling you these things are good. But calling your friend's formal dress 'fine' or saying the poem they've been working on really hard is 'fine' can be a sneaky way of saying they are not fine at all.

Or what if you say 'Sally is so FUN!' when you're talking about her coming out with you, but you say it again when asked if she'd be a good candidate for School Captain. You're saying, 'Yes, let's have her' for the outing, but 'No, not a good idea' for the leadership role. *Fun* can connote 'inappropriate' and 'frivolous' sometimes, just as *fine* can connote 'not good enough' sometimes. It all depends on the context.

Once you're aware that words mean more than just their dictionary definition, you can see fine grades of meaning that are hinted at, but not said directly. This is very important for understanding literature, as well as for being a good writer yourself.

If I say 'He clawed his way to the top', I'm suggesting something animal-like about his path to success. He might be brutal; he might have been (metaphorically speaking) grubbing around in the dirt; or the climb may have been so hard, and he was so determined, that he hung on even with his (metaphorical) fingernails. Whatever the details, it doesn't sound like getting the top job was easy.

If, on the other hand, I say 'He just sailed to the top', you get the idea that not much effort or mucking around on the ground with torn fingernails was required. No, sir! This man has been smoothly delivered from wherever he started to the top, no problems at all.

Allusion

An allusion is a reference to something which is known from a reader's past experience. It doesn't have to be your own personal experience. Allusions are often to stories and things that we know from our cultural heritage, from history or the fairy tales and myths that have come to us over the generations. You know what it means if someone is called a Good Samaritan or a Romeo, even though you might not know the Bible story or

Shakespeare's play. You may know what a Trojan internet virus is – but do you know that it comes from the Greek story of the Trojan Horse? (This should be a Greek virus if the analogy was being used properly. In the original story, Greek soldiers were hidden inside a huge wooden horse presented as an offering to their enemy, the Trojans. By night the tricky Greeks burst out of the horse, opened the city gates and let in the rest of their army. Next step? Slaughter and ruin.)

An allusion is a shortcut, a way to suggest something without explaining it in detail.

Hyperbole

This is an exaggeration that is so dramatic that no one would believe it's true. It's great for threats and insults. (It's also one of the few Greek rhetorical terms that has survived to the present day.)

'He's at death's door' is an overstatement (and also a metaphor).

'I'll crush you underfoot'. Most unlikely.

'They made a heap of money'. Nice for them, but an inconvenient storage method.

Idiom

This is a common figure of speech whose meaning is different from the literal meaning of its words. Worse, it's so different from the dictionary meaning that you can't figure out the meaning on your own.

'Hold your tongue' does not mean 'hold your tongue', it means 'stop talking'. 'Raining cats and dogs' has nothing to do with animals. 'Over the moon' is a physical impossibility, and 'under the weather' poses a similar challenge. Other languages also have confusing expressions which leave you stranded and clueless as to what they are trying to say.

If French speakers say 'The carrots are cooked', they mean the situation can't be changed. And when Russians say 'You can sharpen an axe on the top of his head', they are telling you someone is very stubborn.

Imagery

This means words or phrases a writer uses to create a picture in the reader's mind. Imagery is often based on the five senses.

> Twigs crack. A possum's eyes glint. The earth smells damp. It sinks underfoot as we creep through the night-dark bush.

Euphemisms

Euphemisms disguise the truth of what's going on. They cover for something that is considered distasteful or unpleasant. Euphemisms are often about bodily functions, death or anything that could be embarrassing.

We use euphemisms to shield ourselves from something nasty, or to discuss something which is impolite, off limits or might give offence. We also use euphemisms to make things sound better than they are.

The word *toilet* is a great example of this. To avoid talking about our bowels and bladders, we have almost a whole dictionary's worth of ways not to use the words *urinate* and *defecate*.

Toilet was originally a French word that meant a small piece of cloth, which was – eventually – used to cover a lady's dressing table, the place where she kept her powders and combs and hairpins and whatnot.

The device we call a toilet today was originally called a water closet, or WC.

By the 19th century in America, a small 'toilet room' for tidying yourself up in was provided in some public buildings, and it contained the WC. The rest is history.

Bizarrely we have now euphemised the euphemism, so that a public toilet is called a *convenience*, a *little girls'* or *boys' room*, a *bathroom* or – worse still – a *restroom*. If you need a bath or a rest you know where to go. If you need a pee, it is not so obvious.

Other common euphemisms are ways of not saying *died*, which is, of course, a very unhappy thing. Instead we say a person *passed away* or *passed on, has gone to meet her maker, is now with the angels*. If we're being light hearted we can say *croaked, kicked the bucket* or *bit the dust*.

If you are *economical with the truth*, you have told a lie.

If you are offered *early retirement* or your employer is *downsizing*, you are being made redundant (unnecessary, no longer needed).

Second-hand goods are not *used*, they are *pre-loved* or *pre-owned*.

Renovator's delight is a house that's a broken-down wreck.

Clichés

Clichés are well-worn, familiar expressions that are used so often that they have grown tired and unimaginative. You therefore should give them a miss. The trouble is that it's easier said than done (oops, just used a couple). Clichés got to be clichés by being true, and useful, and easy to remember, and because they work well.

Clichés are **figures of speech**, part of the family of techniques we use to write and speak engagingly, making our meaning clear and our words interesting and enjoyable. Be extremely cautious with them though – they are often the sign of a tired mind.

Shakespeare invented many expressions that have become clichés: *green-eyed monster, cold comfort, heart of gold, in a pickle, love is blind*, to name a few.

I can easily write a whole paragraph made entirely of clichés:

> To prove my point, let's get this show on the road before impenetrable fog means that the traffic grinds

to a halt, though that could be a blessing in disguise. We have time on our side, so we should enjoy this calm before the storm. We're on a mission and there's more than meets the eye here, but so long as we bite the bullet and take the bull by the horns in the nick of time, we can make hay while the sun shines. We're looking for a needle in a haystack and only time will tell if it's rags or riches but one thing's for certain – it won't be a piece of cake.

Clichés don't only apply to words; we also have clichéd situations. They are convenient plots, with stereotyped characters, easy coincidences and well-worked settings. My 'pet hates' are anything that starts or ends with a dream, stories where the unpopular dweeby kid has super-powers, or anything with an artist / writer staring at a blank canvas / computer screen.

Some professions communicate in clichés all the time. Schools want to educate 'global citizens' so they 'engage in empowerment' and 'capacity building'. They want you to 'make a difference' so they 'take you to the next level' by 'pushing you outside your comfort zone'. OK – but what will you actually DO?

Jargon

Jargon is terminology used in specific situations and understood only by a certain group. These are often professional, sporting, activity based or social groups.

You've probably got some jargon in your school, friendship group, taekwondo class or sports team. These groups build their own set of words and phrases that are not understood outside the group. Insiders know exactly what's going on, but no one else. It's not quite a secret society, though to an outsider it can feel that way.

Jargon can be specialised technical language, for example in IT, science or medicine. It can also be 'ordinary' words used in special situations.

If you're a surfer (I'm not) terms like *out the back*, *gnarly*, *nose riding* and *bottom turning* will make sense. They are mystifying to a non-surfer. If you're a cook, you will be comfortable with *springform pans*, *folding egg-whites* and *baking blind*. Non-cooks may wonder what's going on.

Jargon can also be a way of glorifying or raising something's status. The idea is that if it needs a special vocabulary it must be important. When a *suspected perpetrator proceeds rapidly in a southerly direction on foot*, a police officer is saying that the suspect has 'run off that-a-way', but the fancy language dignifies the event and makes sure it does not sound like ordinary conversation.

And that is the point. Jargon can be used to exclude people and hide meaning. If you can't understand me, then you're not 'one of us'.

Be careful to use jargon only when you're sure your whole audience will follow it.

Part 3: How to be a good writer

Manipulative language and bias

There are very good reasons for understanding how to write persuasively, and we have a whole section on persuasion later in the book. But sometimes a piece of writing takes persuasion too far, and misleads you in order to *force* you to believe something (something that's good for the writer). It's done by stealth – not making it obvious. This is called **manipulative language**. The technique involves twisting and distorting information, only telling part of a story, not allowing opposition and closing the door on disagreement or discussion. It's often highly emotional and aimed at our fears. You can call it unreasonable – because reason doesn't play any part in it.

Here's a totally preposterous, manipulative cry for help to fight something that doesn't exist. Someone wants to spook you into giving them your money:

> Aliens are everywhere among us. They seep inside their hosts and lurk, invisible, hiding, ready to attack and kill when they receive the command. You could be hosting one right now! Scientists and governments know all about this but to avoid panic they keep their knowledge secret. This hush-up must stop. Can you live with yourself if you do nothing? Join our anti-alien campaign today. Just $25 per month and you're helping to save the world.

Drafting and writing

Being manipulative is closely related to being biased. **Bias** puts a slant on things. Biased information works for the benefit of one side and ignores anything that would contradict this position. A biased person plays favourites and is not even-handed, neutral or fair in their judgements.

Bias can be hard to spot, as sometimes it's hidden behind attitudes that are (or were) 'normal'. You might not pick up that a writer is biased in favour of men for example, or white people, or a particular religion, because at the time or in the place they wrote, everybody shared the same bias, so they took it to be normal.

In your own writing, you should be sure that you understand the connotations of the words you use. There's a chance that you might have biases of your own. Make sure you say what you mean to say!

 **NERD'S CORNER**

Word origin

The word *bias* is a good example of how figurative language develops. The word literally applies to the weave in fabric. Normal woven material has two threads that form a cross-hatch pattern. If you pull the woven fabric on the diagonal, however, you will find it stretches. The fact that it is not straight, but slanted and stretchy, not firm, gives you an idea of what the word *biased* means.

Essential figurative techniques

Here is a basic list of language techniques which you should learn. They all involve some type of connotation.

Simile

Something is like something else. The words *like* or *as* are needed. Two things are **similar**.

> The kitten stuck to her like a burr.
>
> His face was like a dropped pie.
>
> She was mad as a cut snake.

Note that it's the quality of the second thing that lets us know what to think of the first thing. It's one thing to have *eyes like diamonds*; quite another to have *eyes like a shattered windscreen*.

Metaphor

This goes one step further – one thing IS another thing.

> Love is a battlefield.
>
> The sea is a savage beast.
>
> Juliet is the sun.

A **sustained metaphor** spreads out a rug, unpacks a picnic and settles down. It can last a whole paragraph, poem or an entire story. In the last case, this extreme version of a sustained metaphor is called allegory. The story being told is just the surface. It's a long metaphor for an entirely different story. Spoiler alert: *Animal Farm* is not really about animals, it's about the Russian Revolution. *The Lion, the Witch, and the Wardrobe* is a religious allegory with Aslan as Jesus.

Personification

This is when you give something that is not a person the qualities of a person, hence, *person*ification.

> The stars threw down their spears.
>
> A sunset white and staring.
>
> Great frowning rocks guarded us boldly on either side.
>
> The wind breathes cold.

Onomatopoeia

These words sound like the things they describe:

> *squelch, sizzle, pop, ping, burp*

You won't want much onomatopoeia in formal writing, but there are lots of words that are onomatopoeic in every day speech – *sneeze*, for example. In its early form, *sneeze* was spelled with an *f*, not an *s*. Try and say that! Pretty easy to see the onomatopoeia in action.

Rhythm

Feel the beat of the words. This is especially important in poetry. Tap with your fingers as you speak or read. The writer may be using jagged-edged words: 'gunshots cracked and the silence split'; or long and lazy ones: 'the moon lay low on the horizon'. See what effect the rhythmic pattern is having.

Alliteration

Words that begin with the same sound. NOT NECESSARILY WITH THE SAME LETTERS!! The repetition of that sound creates a web of connection between the words so they are nice to say, and help to make the image memorable.

> Over the cobbles he clattered and clashed.

> A philosophical father figure.

> The fair breeze blew, the white foam flew.

Have you noticed that there are lots of alliterated names for shops, and products? Coca-Cola, Dunkin' Donuts, Krispy Kreme and PayPal – that's because they're so easy to remember.

Drafting and writing

Assonance

This is internal rhyme, where the middle of words sound alike. The 'rhyme is in the line'. It's always important to notice what kind of rhyme it is. If it's long and slow, or short and sharp, for instance – the result is quite different.

> In the walls of the halls where falls
> The tread
> Of the feet of the dead ...
>
> (Hilaire Belloc, 'Tarantella')

> The jaws that bite, the claws that catch!
> ...
> He took his Vorpal sword in hand;
> ...
> One, two! One, two! And through and through
>
> (Lewis Carroll, 'Jabberwocky')

 GIVE IT A GO

Have a look at these examples. What is the author trying to say? What language technique is chosen, and why?
> This morning seems like a lifetime ago.
> The cameras watched like vultures on the traffic lights.
> His speech was on fire.
> Again they went to bed with stomachs growling.
> She goes with slow steps to the barrier.

Modality

Modality is like a scale, with 'certainty' and 'forcefulness' (**high modality language**) at one end, and 'possibility' and 'maybe-ness' (**low modality language**) at the other end.

I've included the word 'language' in that label because modality is a concept that exists in other subject areas as well – it's broadly about the way something is done.

In English it's a way to express how necessary or possible something is (or is not). The most common words expressing modality are:

would / wouldn't, should / shouldn't, could / couldn't, may / may not, might / might not

must, will, need to, have to

possible, probable, certain

possibly, probably, certainly

possibility, probability, certainty

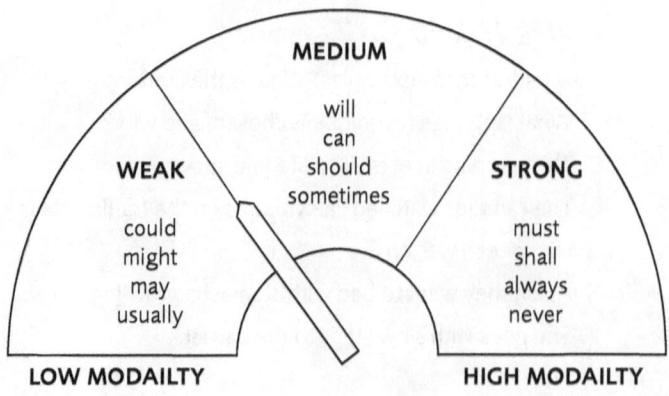

3

EDITING AND PROOFREADING

Editing and proofreading are related, but different, activities.

It's difficult to do either of them to your own work. You know what you wanted to write, and so you will see it there. Even though there may be mistakes, you will overlook them. The best thing is to get someone else to check your work for you. Here are some key things to look for.

Editing

- Do you need all the words you've written? Probably not. Chop out the 'padding', words that don't do much work.
- Remove repetition.
- Cut out those useless words we use from habit: *actually*, *very*, *seriously* – to name just a few.

- Is it arranged logically? Does the structure make sense?
- Does your introduction set the reader up properly?
- Is there a conclusion?
- Have you made any slip-ups with your language registers? Does your work fit the audience, the context and its purpose as it should?
- Do the sentences show variety in length and form, and the way they start?

Proofreading

- Check for spelling and typographical errors. (The computer does a lot of this for you with spellcheck, but don't depend on it. You are still the one responsible for what you write.)
- Check the layout and paragraphing.
- Any punctuation errors? Capitals, full stops, speech marks … all good?
- Have you read it aloud? Reading aloud is the best mistake-finder there is. Try it, and be amazed!

Problems and common mistakes

DO NOT DO THESE!

Could of – would of – should of

NOOOOO! If you write this it's a serious mistake. It shows you don't really know what you're saying. When you speak you say 'should've, would've, could've', but the apostrophe is replacing a missing *ha* in the word *have*, not the preposition *of*. Break it open. You are really saying 'should *have*', 'would *have*', 'could *have*'. There is no verb *of*.

Promise me you will NEVER make this mistake. It's just as bad as writing *gunna* for 'going to' or using *like* every second word. You wouldn't do that, like – would you?

Fewer – less

This mistake is made so widely that it will soon be time to take it off the 'mistakes' list. The rule is:

- Use *fewer* when you're talking about something that's **countable**, and
- *less* when the thing is **uncountable**.

> I'd like less milk please.

There are fewer tickets for the football than we expected.

You can hear this mistake any day of the week in many conversations, even by people who are supposed to set standards – like broadcasters.

It's – its

This usually occurs not because people don't understand what to do, but because they FORGET what to do, thus shortening the tempers and perhaps even the lives of their teachers. If you read about apostrophes on pages 121–122 you know how to solve this one. However, in rapid writing people simply get mixed up and don't stop to think.

It's with an apostrophe is short for *it is* or *it has*.

Its with no apostrophe is the possessive form of the third person pronoun.

> It's raining, so we'd better give the cat its dinner indoors.

Who's – whose

It's the same syndrome: *'s* means you could instead say *who is* or *who has*. But *whose* is a possessive pronoun.

> Whose cap is this?

> Who's coming to the beach?

There – there's – their – theirs – they're

These are the pinnacle of **avoidable spelling mistakes**. They are like quintuplets: five almost identical sounding words, but each with a different use.

Here's how to get them right. Stop and ask yourself, 'What words could replace the one I am thinking of using?'

There has the word *here* buried inside it. That's how you remind yourself that if it refers to a place it's *there*.

If you say *there's* with an *'s* you mean *there is* or *there has*. The apostrophe replaces the missing letters. Note that the missing *is* or *has* is singular. It is not right to say 'There's ants in the jelly'. OK, maybe there ARE ants in the jelly. That's a big enough problem without getting the grammar wrong. Sadly, I hear people making this mistake all the time, so I think this is one of those rules that's going down the grammar plughole.

Their is the third person plural possessive pronoun. It shows that a group of people owns something.

> Their bus came late. Their feet are tired. Their school beat ours.

They're is a contraction of *they are*.

> They're winning!

Your – you're

And here are nearly identical twins that are often confused. Remember:

Your is a possessive pronoun. Your book, your house, your bike.

You're is a contraction of *you are*. You're crazy, you're next, you're my friend.

Between – among

Among is used when you are talking about a group of three or more things. *Between* is for just two things. It's a disagreement *between* a couple, but a disagreement *among* the class.

The tense trap

We went through this on page 43. Don't switch tense in the middle of a piece of writing. It's a bad habit, of young writers in particular.

> Getting to sleep was the hardest part, with all the gunshots. When we wake up it is worse …

> I'm swimming up and I see something just before I got to the top of the water …

While it's true that some writers do move about between tenses, they are usually skilled professionals. As a student you should play it safe. A marker is going to see mixed-up tenses as a sign that your writing is not under control.

Run-on sentences and comma splices

If you write two independent clauses in a sentence, but don't connect them with the right punctuation, it's called a **run-on sentence**. If you put a comma where a full stop or a semicolon should go, to break two independent clauses up, it's called a **comma splice** (from the way you can splice two pieces of rope together). The comma is connecting two sentence parts. Both are mistakes.

These errors are common. The trouble is, we say things like that all the time. It's only a problem for the written word. Picking these errors up takes quite a lot of effort. As the two clauses probably have a connection in meaning, the fact that they're not joined properly may not be obvious. Here's a case study:

> Girls could play in boys' sport teams, the only things stopping them are strength and size.

There are three ways to fix this.

1   Insert a conjunction between the clauses:

> Girls could play in boys' sport teams, <u>but</u> the only things stopping them are strength and size.

2   Insert punctuation between the clauses:

>   Girls could play in boys' sport teams. The only things stopping them are strength and size.

3   Rearrange the sentence:

>   If it weren't for their strength and size, girls could play in boys' sport teams.

Subject–verb agreement

When the subject (doer) in a sentence is singular, the verb matches it and is also singular.

>   I run every day. She runs every day.

It would be wrong to say 'They runs every day'.
When the subject (doer) in a sentence is plural, the verb is also plural.

>   That cake tastes great.

>   Those cakes taste great.

'That cake taste great' is wrong.

Dangling participles

A dangling modifier (often a **dangling participle**) is an ambiguous grammatical construction which means the reader can't tell which word relates to which. The subject of the verb may be unstated, unclear or too far away. It matters because it stops the sentence being understood. It's a depressingly common problem, and an easy mistake to make.

Shakespeare did it:

> Sleeping in mine orchard, a serpent stung me.
> (*Hamlet*)

But you should not. It's often due to misused '-ing' words, so be careful around those.

> Marvelling at the view, the birds began singing.

Are you telling me the birds were marvelling at the view? I think not.

> The thief ran away from the car still holding the keys.

You mean to say 'The thief, still holding the keys, ran away from the car'. Big hint: a car has no hands to hold keys with.

> Squatting in the car park, the delivery van nearly hit me.

Who was squatting? The van or you?
Watch out for this sort of thing in student essays:

> While still focusing on the book, the movie is a major piece of work.

Is the movie focusing on the book? Or do you mean to say 'While the book is our focus, the movie is also a major piece of work'?

{ PART 4 }

WRITING FOR MARKS

Let's face it. You want to do well in tests.

You should feel a bit sorry for your examiners. They have to read billions of words written by students, and their work is quite negative. They have to hunt down the faults. Let's brighten their lives by not having too many faults.

Do you realise that there's a key, a recipe for telling you exactly what you have to do? It's not even a secret. A smart student looks at the marking criteria (called the rubric) to discover what a marker expects to see. Find out what they're looking for and do that!

Most schools (and universities) provide these on a task-by-task basis. For public exams and school-leaving exams, they are available through the website of your local Education Authority.

1
GRADES EXPLAINED

Papers are graded A–F (or something like that), so a marker has to decide what level to place you in.

Marking guides often use words like *elementary, basic, competent, good, excellent* to distinguish between one level and another. So the question becomes, what *is* elementary, what *is* good, what *is* excellent?

A top answer

At the top level – let's call it **excellent** – the writing will be clear, the vocabulary precise, the sentences fluent. These writers are in control and they have plenty to say, so the answer will be complete, detailed and accurate. There will be hardly any errors. They make good use of quotes and evidence. They embed these in their writing seamlessly, and can explain why they are important. These writers see and create connections and patterns between ideas. They can 'join dots' that others may not have noticed. They use language cleverly. Their sentences can be complex, using several clauses and well-chosen connecting words. They use imagery and figurative language to good effect. They are easy to understand, convincing and believable. Their work might even be dazzling. Top-level writers show talent. They have original, fresh ideas and they write them skilfully.

A very good answer

At the next level – let's call it **very good** – writers still have strong skills. They answer the question properly and in depth. Their ideas relate well to each other, and there's one big idea connecting the whole piece. They go deep and explain well, but their insights or creative ideas may be more predictable than those at the top level, and not so original. They might not be perfectly fluent. Their quotations and evidence may seem a bit forced. The vocabulary and the structure of sentences and paragraphs will be good, but not as sophisticated or well-crafted as the best. Figurative language will be simpler and less imaginative.

An acceptable answer

One level down we are looking at a **competent** performance. These writers do what they're supposed to do. Their meaning is clear. Their answers may be a bit shorter because they don't drill down into the issues they're dealing with, and so they don't develop and expand as much as they could. Their ideas and the way they express them are simpler. Their writing may not have a lot of detail. In a creative piece, they might adapt another's idea, rather than inventing their own material. In an analytical piece, they might recount too much of the work they are writing about, rather than getting on with the analysis and commentary. They might not use quotes and evidence well, perhaps using too few, or ones that are not relevant. They may not find quite the right words, and their syntax could be unclear or confusing.

Not quite there yet

Developing writers don't manage long answers because their ideas are not expanded or filled out. They may use clichés and predictable words and phrases. The structure of sentences and paragraphs may be disorderly and illogical. There will be errors in spelling and punctuation, as well as in sentence and paragraph construction. They may have limited vocabulary, and use simple language. They tend to write simple stories or persuasive pieces which do not use examples and evidence well.

THREE ASSESSMENT FORMATS

There are three major types of writing for exams and assessments. We're going to look at each one in detail. We'll begin with **creative writing**, then look at **persuasive writing** and finally **analytical writing**. The approaches outlined here reflect the way each piece of writing would be assessed and marked in a big exam.

2
CREATIVE WRITING

This is what it sounds like. You are the creator. It's all yours to make up and write down. You invent it. The form you most often use in school is called **narrative writing**, which means writing 'a story'. But creative writing can also include poetry, or a script for a play or a film. Let's work through the essentials for creative writing.

Genre

Narrative writing is mostly fiction, and you'll know it from reading novels – they are all narratives. Many stories follow typical plots and have predictable settings, characters and language styles. This is called **genre**. There are far too many genres to name, but a few examples are fantasy, science, horror, gothic, romance, detective, thriller, adventure and dystopian fiction. (Turn to pages 257–260 if you'd like a rundown of the key ingredients in the major genres.) You are free to base your writing on any of these genre types if you want to.

There is another species of narrative writing, which is non-fiction. It's based on facts and real events, but they are presented as a story. The story is a true one, not made entirely out of the writer's imagination. If you've read the story of someone's life, or a book about 'my hero', or a story of something that happened in history, that's **narrative non-fiction**.

Ideas

You are often given a **stimulus** as a starting idea for your creative writing. It could be a picture, or an audio or film clip, a news item, advertisement or letter. You could also be given some text as a 'story starter' (for example, the title or the opening lines).

Study the stimulus. Try to figure out what could have led to this – what made this happen? Use the stimulus as a springboard, but don't abandon it once you've started writing. You need to work it in properly so that it has a role in your writing.

Planning your work

Turn your computer OFF.

On separate bits of paper, post-it notes, a whiteboard, or in a mindmap – whatever works for you – write any ideas down. If you can identify a main idea, write it down and circle it. Write down all the ideas that spring into your head until you can think of nothing new. Don't worry about whether they're any good, just do a nice big brain dump.

Look for 'families' of ideas – ones that relate to each other. See if there are possible links between your ideas. Try to sort them into groups where they all fit in logically with one other, the way branches do on a tree.

In a creative piece you should aim for three major branches, which are all equally important:

1 The plot – what happens and why
2 The setting – where it happens
3 The characters – who it happens to.

Now sort your ideas into 'must have' and 'could have'. Cross out or throw out what you can. If you realise something important is missing, add it in.

Now get ready to write.

 WISE ADVICE

Young writers sometimes think 'story' is the same as 'plot' and get very busy writing events. This is a mistake. The characters and setting matter just as much. My advice is that you should work on character – who is in the story – well before you start working out the plot.

Part 4: Writing for marks

Here are some student story plans.

She goes to her wonderland every day
magical orb controls the hand.
It is taken by the hunters and all life is lost. She
sneaks in and is captured one of the hunters lets
her out and she is free.

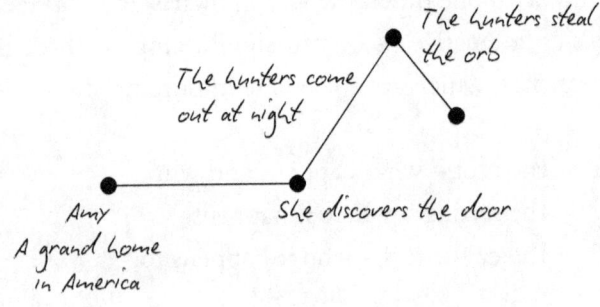

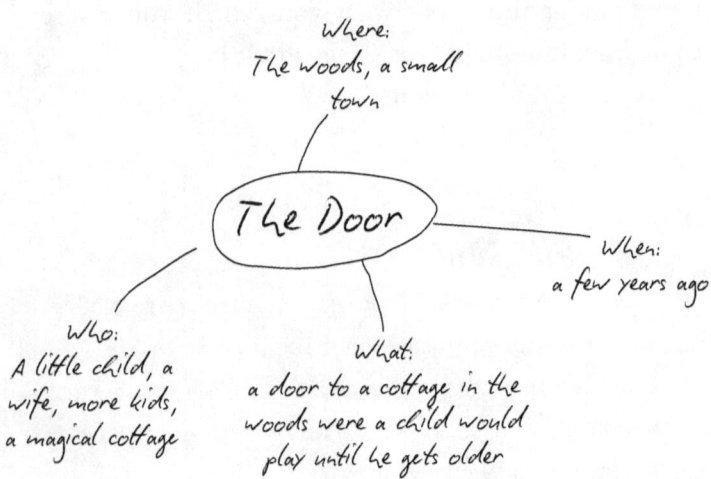

NERD'S CORNER

Famous writers' plans

Google 'well-known writers planning' to find examples of how successful novelists plan their work. The notes that J.K. Rowling drew up for her books are well worth a look.

Creating a character

To make a character believable, you must think about their inner nature, the sort of person they really are and how this will appear to the reader.

You also need to know their relationships to others in the story, and what life-defining things may have happened to them before the story starts. It's very common, for instance, for children in stories to be orphans, with no pesky parents to boss them about – an obvious way of creating a world where the kids can take charge.

You need their appearance, mannerisms, their personality and the way they talk. What would a person like this say and do?

All these aspects of character need to match each other. You may not use all the information in your story, but having it in your head will help you to round your characters out and make them believable.

Now you've got that sorted, here are three ways to bring your characters to life.

Part 4: Writing for marks

> 👀 **WISE ADVICE**
>
> If you are really serious about writing, you'll keep a little notebook in your pocket and jot down things you overhear, or see people do. This is like a pantry cupboard of stuff you can use in stories some time in the future.

Use nouns and adjectives

To create a convincing character you need **nouns**, **noun phrases** and **adjectives**. They're underlined here.

> John Reed was a <u>schoolboy of fourteen years old</u> … <u>large</u> and <u>stout</u> for his age, with a <u>dingy</u> and <u>unwholesome</u> skin … <u>heavy limbs</u> and <u>large extremities</u>.

Hmm. I don't think John Reed is going to be our hero. Here, by contrast, IS the hero of the novel:

> He had a <u>dark face</u>, with <u>stern features</u> and a <u>heavy brow</u> … he was <u>past youth</u>, but had not reached middle age; perhaps he might be thirty-five. I felt no fear of him.

Often, we expect a character with a stern, dark face to have a cold, dark heart. But in that simple last sentence we are proved wrong. Now we are curious. There is something scary, yet safe, about this man. We want him explained.

Those sentences were written almost two hundred ago by Charlotte Brontë, whose novel *Jane Eyre* is so realistic and gripping that it is still one of the mightiest in the English language.

I have a list of hundreds of words that can be used to describe characters. Let me throw just a few of them at you now: *indecisive, inventive, intrepid, jolly, judgemental, knowledgeable, lazy, lovable, materialistic, melancholy, monstrous, nonchalant, opinionated, patient, personable, pompous*. I could go on, but I think you get the idea.

Googling 'other ways to say' is a great way to find new words to describe people and things. You may not even use the words you find, but they will stimulate your ideas and help you to think about what a character can be like. They'll help you to round your characters out and make them believable.

Dialogue makes it real

Direct speech is your best tool for making a story feel immediate, as though you are really present. It works by letting the characters reveal themselves in the words they say.

Dialogue is strictly for advancing the plot and revealing character. Don't waste words on the kind of chitter-chatter and half-sentences you have in real life.

Use speech marks properly. Start a new line for every switch in speaker.

Here is Sherlock Holmes, excited about a new test for blood. How do we know he's excited? Because of the rapid, short sentences (which provide considerable information) and the pile of questions which builds tension until the climax, the 'reveal'. It's as if he said 'Ta-da!!' before the last sentence.

> 'Criminal cases are continually hinging upon that one point. A man is suspected of a crime months perhaps after it has been committed. His linen or clothes are examined, and brownish stains discovered upon them. Are they blood stains, or mud stains, or rust stains, or fruit stains, or what are they? That is a question which has puzzled many an expert, and why? Because there was no reliable test. Now we have the Sherlock Holmes' test, and there will no longer be any difficulty.'
>
> (Arthur Conan Doyle, *A Study in Scarlet*)

Characters should change

A story is a journey, and the main characters should grow and change – or maybe learn something new – by the time it ends. Characters ought to develop as the story unfolds, and the reader should be barracking for them. If you've written characters we like, we will want to see them get something they want. Maybe they survive a setback, break some rules, fulfil an ambition, find out a truth or achieve a goal. Maybe they accept a loss, or a sadness, and learn to live with it. Maybe they get to live the dream.

Harry Potter matures and gains faith in himself by facing his enemies. Katniss Everdene of *The Hunger Games* takes on a new identity and changes her personality so she can survive. Cinderella goes from being a lonely downtrodden orphan to marrying the Prince and living happily ever after.

In the planning stage you should think through what the big shift will be. Note down the main points of how your principal character will grow from start to finish.

The plot

Some people say there are only a few basic plots. Someone gets into trouble, then gets out of it. An ordinary day turns out to be wonderful. Someone overcomes a monster or goes on a quest. The underdog turns into the top dog. You can easily use these storylines. Whether you do or not, your plot will have six main steps.

Six steps to a great story

1 An **introductory section** lets the reader know where they are and what's happening. The reader needs to understand who, what, when, where.

2. A **complication**. Think of this as 'the bomb' (💣*) because it's just as if someone's thrown one into the story. Everything is disrupted. It doesn't actually have to be a massive explosion; it could be quite gentle and understated. But whatever it is, it's like kicking a ball into play. It sets the story off.

3. After the complication, we get what is called **rising action**. A series of events triggered by 'the bomb' progressively creates more tension. Obstacles get in the way of the main character's getting what they want. Things get tougher and stickier and more difficult.

    In a short piece of writing, the rising action may consist of two or three events. In a longer piece (a novel, for example), the rising action could take three steps forward and two steps back, four steps forward and one step back ... over many chapters.

4. At the **climax**, things come to a head. The situation becomes intolerable. We can't take any more. This tension must be released. The problems come together in a confrontation or show-down of some kind, which sorts it all out. This is the turning point.

5. After the crisis of the climax comes the **resolution**. It might be a happy ending, or it might not be, but you need to ease back down and show how the situation is resolved. In the process, you write a closing section for the story and bring it all to ...

6   A satisfying **conclusion**. The story should end with all the loose ends tied up. Don't leave us wondering about what happened to this character or that. The bomb and its aftermath should all be tidied away and wrapped up neatly. The characters' journeys are over and they are now different from the way they were at the start. Whether the story is happy, sad or somewhere in between, the reader should feel it has come to a satisfying close.

Here is a diagram showing this. Notice that the closing section (the resolution) balances the rising tension. It may not always be as long, but it still takes quite a bit of space. This is important for giving your story balance. Too many young writers get to the climax, go blank, and write 'The End'.

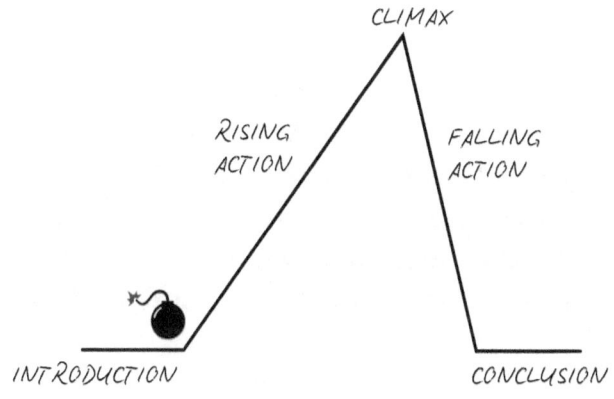

Part 4: Writing for marks

> **WARNING!**
> You won't impress anyone if your plot seems a lot like someone else's; or if it relies on schlock, melodrama, catastrophe, the zombie apocalypse, blood and guts, interplanetary travel or unexpected, unexplained explosions. Don't write anything violent or gross. And no waking up at the end and discovering it was all a dream.

Great openers

Here are the openings of some famous, classic books. It's impressive how quickly they let us know where we are, when, why and who with. I've made some notes on what caught my attention.

Riverside – leisurely

Alice was beginning to get very tired of sitting by her sister on the bank, and of having <u>nothing to do</u>: once *Lazy day* or twice she had peeped into the book her sister was reading, but it had no pictures or conversations in it, 'and what is the use of a book,' thought Alice 'without pictures or conversations?' *Bored, wants excitement*

(Lewis Carroll, *Alice in Wonderland*)

Creative writing

Flashback

<u>Heavy-footed</u> — I remember him as if it were yesterday, as he came plodding to the inn door, his <u>sea-chest</u> following behind
<u>Sunburned sailor</u> — him in a hand-barrow – a tall, strong, heavy, <u>nut-brown man</u>, his <u>tarry pigtail falling</u> over the shoulder of his — *Olden days*
<u>Filthy</u> — <u>soiled blue coat</u>, his <u>hands ragged and scarred</u>, with *Rough hands* black, broken nails, and <u>the sabre cut across one cheek</u>, *SCARFACE!* a dirty, livid white. *Old, tough sailor with an unknown past.*

Robert Louis Stevenson, *Treasure Island*)

Deprivation

<u>There was no possibility</u> of taking a walk that day. We had been <u>aimless</u>, <u>lost</u>, indeed, in the <u>leafless</u> shrubbery *Barren* an hour in the morning; but since dinner (Mrs. Reed, when there was no company, dined early) the <u>cold</u>
Bleak <u>winter wind</u> had brought with it <u>clouds so sombre</u>, and *Dark*
No let-up a <u>rain so penetrating</u>, that further out-door exercise was now out of the question. *Dismal, gloomy place*

(Charlotte Brontë, *Jane Eyre*)

👀 WISE ADVICE

Although it's a good idea to write stories based on your own experience (so you know what you're talking about), there is a risk that you will just retell events, without giving them the shape (that pattern of tension and release) that goes into telling a story really well. So it could be boring. 'First we ... then we ... and after that we ... before too long we ...'. Yawn! Even if you are writing from life, put your imagination to work, and rearrange, add or leave things out in order to create a storyline.

WARNING!

Don't overcomplicate your plot. It can easily get hectic. Just a few incidents are plenty for a short story. Be original; no ripoff plots! You're not the only one who knows *The Matrix*, *Harry Potter*, *Fortnite*, *Game of Thrones* – or whatever the current cult is.

Setting

The reader needs to know where they are in place and time. Creating a well-thought-out setting helps us feel we've gone somewhere, as if we get a break from our own lives and have a little holiday in the world that you, the writer, have created for us.

The location of the story is much more than the background. Sometimes it's the setting that makes the story happen. You can't have *Lord of The Rings* without Middle Earth, or Narnia without the frozen land beyond the wardrobe.

Your setting needs to create the right mood. If yours is a scary story, set it at night in a dark and strange place. If it's a mystery, then there might be something odd about the place. What effect would it have if we put a castle in the distance? Or what if it's a forest yet we hear waves? How about being on a seashore that's littered with dead sea birds and plastic?

It's in the detail

When you create a scene, it's the details that make it convincing. Think of Hogwarts. We know so much about every part of it – both the place and the routine of daily life, as well as the characters who live there – that it's almost like another character.

One way to come up with details is to think through each of your senses. What would your character experience in this place? What's the weather like? Is there something they can touch? What do they hear? Anything to taste? Smell? How did they get there? And what do they see?

Fire up your imagination as you read this passage. Which senses does it appeal to? What impression does it make?

> After trudging through long grass for an hour we reached a little weatherbeaten cottage, dwarfed by overgown trees. The sun broke through the clouds just as we arrived, bathing the old cabin in afternoon light. The wind sighed, and an occasional bird call broke the silence. With a deep breath we could smell the sweetness of the old garden, and the mustiness of the house.

We know we are in the country and have come to a place that is quiet, old and holds the promise of something to come.

Part 4: Writing for marks

Here is a description that comes alive because of the details. Note the great verbs and vivid nouns.

> A shimmering summer morning warm and still, with cicadas shrilling ... Heavy headed dahlias flamed and drooped in the immaculate flower beds.
>
> (Joan Lindsay, *Picnic at Hanging Rock*)

And here are three sentences that perfectly describe a crowded slum, a cold place, both literally and figuratively. What does it tell you to have children compared to vermin?

> The golden sunset was waning and the air had grown sharp. A horde of grimy children populated the street. They stood or ran in the roadway, or crawled up the steps before the gaping doors, or squatted like mice upon the thresholds.
>
> (James Joyce, *Dubliners*)

3
PERSUASIVE WRITING

Persuasion means to convince or get someone to do something because you want them to. Earlier in this book we learned about connotation and figurative language. These play an important part in writing persuasively.

These days we're bombarded with sophisticated persuasion (ads, product placement, marketing ...) all the time. It's just part of life. But there are many other forms of persuasion all around you.

When a toddler throws a tantrum to get something they want, that's persuasion. When you hear a speaker raising funds for a charity, that's persuasion. When you try to get your parents to let you go out on a school night, that's persuasion. When a barrister argues a case in court, that's persuasion.

In early high school you will be asked to write persuasively on topics like 'Should students wear uniforms to school?' or 'Should animals be kept in captivity?' These are real issues where points of view differ. There's no right or wrong. As you get older you have to argue about questions that depend more on your knowledge of a subject. Can we blame Romeo and Juliet's parents for their deaths? What were the causes of the First World War? What are the pros and cons of different energy sources?

Ethos, pathos and logos

If we take a look at persuasion over time, we see that while topics and language may change, the basic principles being used do not. That's good news. It's these principles that I want you to learn.

About 2300 years ago, Aristotle (an ancient Greek philosopher) wrote a book called *The Art of Rhetoric*. This book has been so important that it is still a reference today. In it he said there were three secrets to being persuasive. Being Greek, he called them *ethos*, *pathos* and *logos*. In English you might think of them as *character*, *connection* and *content*. Together they are known as the **rhetorical triangle**.

Inside those three Greek words you can see some modern English ones.

- *Ethos* leads you to *ethical*. That's 'rightness'. It's a moral quality, to do with what we value and think is proper, what we should do or say, think or believe. Think 'character'.
- *Pathos*, which in Greek means suffering, emotion

Persuasive writing

or experience, gets you to *pathetic*, *sympathy* and *empathy*. It's about feeling for another, being sensitive, compassionate. Think 'connection'.
- *Logos* leads us to *logic*, and is about the *reason* that lies beneath a persuasive argument. Think well-explained 'content'.

 NERD'S CORNER

Rhetoric

You might already know the word *rhetorical* because you will have heard of **rhetorical questions**. What, I ask you, is a rhetorical question? That was. They are asked for effect, and the answer is understood – it doesn't need to be said. Rhetoric, however, is a much wider subject. It's the art of being an effective speaker or writer. Rhetorical questions are only one of many techniques that persuaders can use.

The rhetorical triangle in action

The rhetorical triangle is like a three-legged stool. All three 'legs' together do a great job. Leave one out and your persuasive powers will fail. You need all three to persuade, and learning to use them is a foundation skill. It will support all the writing you do in school and right on through to university, as well as in other aspects of your life.

In a nutshell, persuasion depends on:

1 Your values: who you are, your position, background, or what you know.
2 Getting the audience onside, into a certain frame of mind.
3 The proof or evidence that's offered.

What you also need, of course, are some good ideas, well arranged, in a style that fits the situation.

Persuasive language

Let's assume you've got a good idea; you know what you want to persuade people about. You're going to need to adjust that persuasive recipe and mix those three key ingredients up.

Which of them – ethos, pathos or logos – should take the lead? Will it work best to be mainly emotional – like the charity fundraiser, who stirs your feelings about social justice and caring for others in order to motivate you to act? Or should you be rational and logical like the barrister, who lets the evidence do most of the work? Would ethical or value-based arguments persuade your parents it's good for you to be out on a weeknight? This is a key decision.

> **WISE ADVICE**
> Make sure that the subject you're writing about, the audience you're writing for and the approach you take, all fit well together. Turn to page 253 for a detailed table that shows you some language features that you can use for each of the three persuasive 'channels'.

Planning a persuasive piece

The process is similar to the one on pages 206–207 for creative writing, though the content is different.

1. Turn your electronic devices OFF. Just think.
2. On separate bits of paper, post-it notes, a whiteboard, or in a mindmap, write down your main idea. Express it as a position: 'You should elect me as school captain'; or 'Romeo and Juliet's parents are to blame for their deaths'; or 'Solar power is the best renewable energy source for Australia'.
3. Then write down all the ideas that spring into your head, and link them to your main idea – like branches on a tree.

All you want at this stage is ideas. Plenty of them. It's a brain dump, so do it fast. Don't stop to think about whether each idea is a good one or not. Just empty your brain as if it were a dump truck.

If you need a prompt to help you, take a look at my 'all-purpose argument maker', a mnemonic (look it up!) based on the word SPEECH (one of the most important forms of persuasion). The idea is that you think about whether there might be issues that fall under any of the headings that make up the list.

Ms Duffy's all-purpose argument maker	**S**ocial
	Political
	Economic
	Environment
	Education
	Cultural
	Historical

When you've got a good supply of ideas – no matter how untidy – review your progress. Check that you've answered the following questions and, if you haven't, go back and add some more points:

- What's the dilemma (or problem) here?
- How do I know it's a dilemma or problem? (This is to help you to find examples, evidence and proof.

You are going to need these, especially examples.)
- What do other people say about this? Why are their opinions wrong, or right?
- What is my solution, answer or opinion?
- Why is mine the best choice or the right way?

Now, sort your material into 'families', looking for links between issues, or themes that relate to each other. These families will each become a paragraph. Read on ...

Writing a persuasive paragraph

PEEL

Here is the best, award-winning, tried-and-true method of building a persuasive paragraph.

P is for **Point**. Begin with a topic sentence – one simple statement that says what the paragraph will be about. At the opening of the essay this is where you give your opinion. (There's more on topic sentences in the section on paragraphs, pages 148 and 238.)

E is for **Expand** on it: **Elaborate**, **Explain**. Say *why* you think what you think. What led you to this view? Use the words *because, when, since, we see how*. Explaining why you think what you think shows your train of thought, how you came to this opinion. It opens your reasoning, or emotional responses, up for examination. That improves our ability to follow and agree with you.

E is for **Evidence**, or **Examples**. Now you must introduce some proof. Use real evidence that fits the point you're making. Many students mistakenly think they need statistics or research – but that's only true in the older years. You can be persuasive by using general, well-known examples, quotes, anecdotes (small stories to illustrate) and also common sense. You want to be believable, true and trustworthy. Phrases like 'It is generally agreed that …'; 'We expect people to …'; 'It's normal to …' can help you out here.

L is for **Link**. End your paragraph by saying what your point is, and then say something which leads in to the next point you are going to discuss.

Here's an example from a young writer:

> **Should school students be able to listen to music in class?**
>
> Music can help you focus but listening to music in class can be bad. As a school student I would love to be able to listen to music in all classes but I know that the right answer is no.
>
> If students were allowed to listen to music in classes they would get easily distracted. When students are distracted they do not complete their work or do not listen to the teacher's instructions. Teachers can get very annoyed with this. For example, if I was writing

Annotations in margins:
- OPINION OVERALL
- EXPAND EXPLAIN
- EXAMPLE EVIDENCE
- Point
- Reason
- Commonsense explanation

Persuasive writing

an essay and some song I didn't like the sound of came on and I wanted to change it, it means I would have to stop what I was doing, click off the essay, change the music and resume my essay, which stops my thinking.

EXAMPLE EVIDENCE

Reason

2nd Point (Opposite point of view)

On the other hand, listening to music could be good (because) some students may feel more comfortable listening to music while in class (because) it may be easier for ideas to spill out on the page. <u>Music may take off some stress and make it easier to work.</u> I believe that it is okay to listen to music in classes like art, or design and technology, (because) music helps you be creative.

EXPAND

Commonsense reason

EXAMPLE EVIDENCE

Reasons

Reason

<u>In conclusion</u>, while working in class students should not be able to listen to music.

Getting the marks

A marker is going to be looking for the following things. Here's your checklist. You should learn it off by heart.

1   Audience: Is your tone right? Did you address them directly? Have you hooked them with a strong start?
2   Structure:
    - Introduction – states your opinion and signposts the issues

- Body – develops persuasive arguments
- Conclusion – wraps it up gracefully.
3 Ideas make sense and are right for the job.
4 Persuasive devices are obvious (there's a list on page 253).
5 Writing skills:
    - well-chosen vocabulary
    - all words correctly spelled
    - well-connected and varied sentences
    - properly punctuated
    - subdivided into paragraphs.

Personal persuasive challenge

Next time you have to write something persuasive, set yourself a target. Choose three, four or five of these persuasive devices and build them into your work.

Adjectives
Adverbs
Anecdotes
Addressing the audience directly (using 'we' or 'you')
Emotional language (for example, high modality, exaggeration, hyperbole)
Punctuation for emphasis
Addressing the opposing view
Offering others' opinions (for example, quoting an expert)

Facts, statistics
Rhetorical questions
Repetition for effect

 GIVE IT A GO

Have a look at these persuasive sentences. Are they arguing from ethos, pathos or logos? Which persuasive device is being used?

> According to a recent survey, 67% of Australians agree.
>
> Professor MacIntyre once described the idea as a 'disgrace'.
>
> Surely, we all agree that this is the right course of action.
>
> The money is a drop in the bucket compared to what government spends on other services.
>
> It's a more humane option.
>
> Can't you do anything right?
>
> It will be the end of civilisation as we know it.
>
> There are a million reasons this idea won't work.
>
> It's a problem that we can't turn away from.
>
> We've been working like dogs to achieve this change.

4
ANALYTICAL WRITING

The third type of writing you do is **analytical writing**. This is similar to persuasive writing in two ways: you must write an essay which explains your opinions and provides evidence to justify them. However, analytical writing is about something that's been created by someone else. You take their work apart, have a good look at its makeup, explain what it means, then tell us how they did it. To do *that* you have to be able to talk about the techniques they've used, and what effects they produce.

Have you ever written a film review? That was analytical. You said whether or not you liked it, but you needed to mention the plot, the way the scenes looked, what sort of camera work was used, the soundtrack, how the actors portrayed the characters, and what overall effect all that had. You can already do it!

For English, analytical writing will likely be about a novel you've studied, or a poem, a film or a TV show. The questions will be things like: Is Shakespeare's Lady Macbeth the 'real' murderer? In what ways is Harper Lee's character Atticus Finch in *To Kill A Mockingbird* courageous? What does the imagery in Robert Frost's poem 'Stopping by Woods on a Snowy Evening' evoke?

For other subjects, your topic could be something to do with history, religion, economics or sport. The range of possibilities is enormous, but in all cases your task is to explore, explain and respond to the question you've been given.

Analytical writing is a complex, high-level skill and you take a long time to develop it. You start work on it in early high school. By the time you're a school leaver you need to be very good at it. As a university student, this is likely to be the main type of writing you'll do for assessments.

Analytical writing step by step

You will be asked a question or given a problem, and your answer needs to be justified. It must be clearly related to the work you are responding to. It's not enough to give an opinion (I really liked that poem!). The reader / marker needs to know *why* you think what you do and, most importantly, *what* it is that led you to think this. You need to dig out the parts of the work that helped you to form your opinion and explain how they did it.

The four key elements for this format are:

1. The main idea (known as the **thesis**)
2. What leads you to have this idea (why your thesis is convincing)
3. Explaining and justifying it – leading the reader through your idea in detail, showing why your idea is strong
4. Proving it with evidence:
   - specific quotes and references
   - naming the language technique that's used in the quote
   - explaining the effect of the technique – what it does for the meaning
   - why *this* quote is a significant one.

Instructional words

But first, let's look closely at what you're being asked to do.

There are instructional words in analytical questions, and they give you directions about how to answer the question properly. Here are some of the terms you're most likely to meet:

Explain	Give reasons, show connections or cause and effect
Analyse	Identify key features, say what effect / result they produce, find relationships and connections

Analytical writing

Evaluate	Judge something; say what's good and bad about it, and how valuable or successful it is
Clarify	Explain so that something is clear
Compare	Show the similarities and differences between two things
Contrast	Show the differences between two things
Define	Identify essential qualities
Identify	Recognise and name
Describe	Say what the main features are
Discuss	Talk about; identify issues and say something about them
Examine	Look closely at and describe main features
Interpret	Say what something means
Justify	Give reasons to support a particular position
Outline	Note the main features
Recount	Retell a series of events
Summarise	Condense, using the most important details
Synthesise	Blend two or more different things together into one

Preparing to write

A great many students get poor marks because they just didn't answer the question. Maybe they answered only part of it, or maybe they answered what they thought the question was.

Once you are clear about what type of information you're being asked for, you must make sure you understand what the question means. To do that takes four steps. DON'T take shortcuts.

Part 4: Writing for marks

1. Look at the wording. Hard.
2. Underline the key words – the ones that carry the most load.
3. Box or circle any words which might have mixed or hidden meanings – words that are open to interpretation. Decide for yourself what these mean in this context, and be prepared to explain.
4. Paraphrase the question. This means write it out in your own words.

Here's a worked example. The question is about Shakespeare's play *The Merchant of Venice*:

> Is Shylock a victim of his times, or a victim of his own character? Discuss both sides of this question and form your own conclusions.

I've underlined the key words and put a box around the term that needs explaining.

> Q: Is Shylock a ⬚victim⬚ of his <u>times</u>, or a <u>victim</u> of his <u>own character</u>? <u>Discuss both sides</u> of this question and <u>form your own conclusions</u>.

Now, here's my paraphrase of the question, with instructions to myself:

> I have to explain what a victim is and show how and why Shylock was persecuted and hated. I must give one or two examples. Talk about (1) how

much this was due to his being a Jew (this was a common attitude to Jews back then); (2) how much it's because he was a cruel, harsh man. Then I must decide which of the two I think is most right and say why.

Developing a thesis statement

A **thesis** is the idea that guides your writing. It's like the spine that holds the whole thing up. Although you state your thesis at the start of your essay (in the introductory paragraph), its influence is felt throughout. When you've finished drafting, look carefully to see whether everything you've written is well connected to the thesis. If it's not, cut it out.

A good thesis is specific, addresses the question directly and does not waffle or generalise. For the question above, a thesis statement (which doubles as an introductory paragraph) could be:

> Shylock is despised by everyone. He is kicked, insulted and taunted by the Christians, and his own daughter betrays him. Persecuting Jews was commonplace when this play was written. However, by hardening himself, and becoming cold and vengeful, Shylock made a bad situation worse for himself.

It would NOT be a good thesis statement to say:

> The persecution of Jews is an age-old historical abuse that is still going on. Shakespeare uses Shylock to show us that Jews are no different from anyone else.

While the points here may be arguable, they don't get you started on answering the actual question.

Analytical paragraph structure

In analytical writing, a paragraph is strictly structured. It has four parts, which are very similar to the PEEL structure we met in persuasive writing (page 227). You should also refresh your know-how on paragraph writing – pages 147–151.

1. It begins with a *topic sentence*, or *point*. That's a simple, clear statement of what the paragraph will be about. It does not have to be lengthy or complicated – in fact, it's best if it isn't. Just a short sentence will do fine. A one-clause sentence is a great paragraph starter and will always do a good job as a topic sentence. Use the opening sentence to state the single idea that controls the coming paragraph. For example:

   > Shylock is a tragic figure.

Analytical writing

If you'd like to upgrade to something more complex, your topic sentence can have two parts. The second part explains, and gives direction to what you're going to say. Use words like *although* or *because*, *due to* or *considering*, to join the two parts together.

> Shylock is a tragic figure, because when he tries to take revenge for the abuse he has suffered, he makes matters much worse.

2. You must expand on this and back it up. Provide *reasons* for why you think what you think. By letting us see inside your mind and exploring, elaborating and adding depth, you build 'believability'. Finding good reasons means asking yourself over and over, 'Why do we care?', 'How do I know this?' and saying 'This matters because …'.

> As a Jew, Shylock can never be socially accepted. A proud but isolated man, he resents the Christians who need his money but show contempt when he gives it to them. No-one respects him and this makes him hate them. He alone knows the truth is that Jews are no different from any other person. He seizes the opportunity for revenge on his tormentors when the chance arises. He decides to give them a taste of their own medicine, but his attempt is doomed.

3   Now you must introduce some supporting *examples*. If you are answering a question about a text you're studying, you'll need quotes that fit the point you're making. It's good to weave these quotes into the reasons you have just written. The two can be blended, like this:

> As a Jew Shylock can never be socially accepted. A proud but isolated man, he resents the Christians who need his loans, yet insult him. "You call me misbeliever, cut-throat dog, And spit upon my Jewish gabardine … it now appears you need my help". Shylock's response to their abuse is to hate them in return: "I hate him for he is a Christian"; and threaten retaliation: "Thou calledst me a dog before thou hadst a cause, But since I am a dog, beware my fangs."
>
> He knows that a Jew is no different from any other person. In court he pleads his cause passionately: "If you prick us, do we not bleed? if you tickle us, do we not laugh? if you poison us, do we not die?" In frustration and anger he decides to pay his persecutors back: "And if you wrong us shall we not revenge?" He wants them to suffer as he has done. "The villainy you teach me I will execute".

Analytical writing

4   Finally, state why this proves your thesis. Summarise what you've said in one sentence using the phrase 'This shows…'., or 'we can see from this…'. When you conclude your paragraph this way, it will click into place in the marker's mind as a well-made point that has been proved. You are also setting up the move to your next paragraph.

> This shows that Shylock's anger and resentment are understandable, but his desire for revenge turns out to be a tragic error. He thinks that he can stand up to his persecutors and win. But he has no power. No one is on his side, and in the end, he loses everything.

 WARNING!

Things not to do
There are two big 'no-nos' when it comes to analytical writing.
- Never retell the story you're writing about.
- Do not describe; always explain.

Comparative essays

Writing an essay that compares two works (for example, a novel, a poem, a movie, a photograph, a poster) is one of the hardest skills students must learn. The challenge of organising your material is as great as the challenge of deciding what to say. Make no mistake, this is a high-level skill.

These are sometimes called **synthesis** essays. Synthesising means making things come together so that two (or more) things merge into one.

Be sure to look carefully at the instructional language so that you present the right information. You will be following the same paragraph structure used for analytical writing. It's also safe to assume that you need an introduction with a thesis, and a short justification for the thesis; and that you will wrap up with one of those graceful conclusions described on page 170.

Structural options

Let's say you've been asked to evaluate which is better entertainment, the book or the film of *Mao's Last Dancer*.

After you've studied and interpreted the question (underlined the key words and paraphrased it), the first issue is to decide what the organising principle of your essay will be. There are three possible approaches.

Analytical writing

1. Compare the whole of one work with the whole of another.
2. Find the similarities between the two works and compare those; then find the differences and compare those.
3. Compare the two works point by point.

A good way to decide which one to choose is to make a Venn diagram, or a three-column chart, showing what the works do and don't have in common. Choose whichever method works best for you.

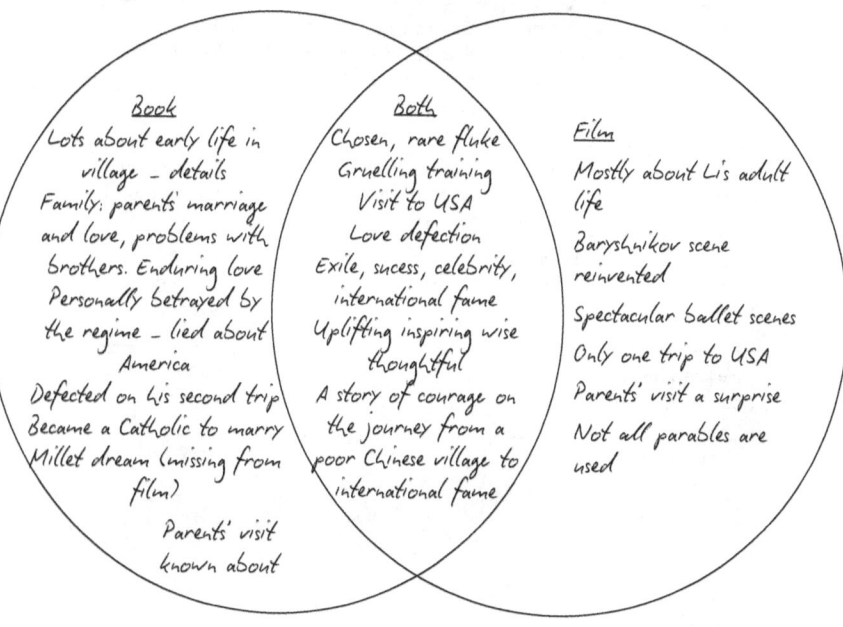

Part 4: Writing for marks

*Mao's Last Dancer*		
Book	**Both**	**Film**
Long: 400 pages		Short: 117 minutes (100 pages of script)
Details of early life – much about living in extreme poverty in his home village, and daily life as he grew up	Selected by a fluke, left home; Beijing dance academy a gruelling experience	Mostly adult experiences
Parents' arranged marriage and strong love; family details, meals, celebrations, coping with poverty, brothers' problems	Attained high standards and was allowed to go to USA	Lots of spectacular dance sequences
Sense of personal betrayal when he learns how the regime deceived him about America	Danced well, fell in love, defected. A highly dramatic and conflict-ridden experience	The Baryshnikov scene is re-imagined
He defected on his second trip	The main story is unchanged: the journey from a Chinese village and poverty to international ballet stardom, via political turmoil, love, duty, exile, family, celebrity and triumph	Defected on his only trip
Converted to Catholicism when he wanted to marry Liz		The Millet dream parable is left out
He knew his parents were coming to Houston		Parents' visit is a surprise

Analytical writing

1 Whole to whole

Here you write everything you wish to say about one work, and then everthing you wish to say about the other. Remember that what you say about the second one must cover the same points you addressed for the first, and in the same order. Therefore, the same issues are covered twice. When writing about the second work, you need to say things like 'just as in [first work]', 'similarly', 'by contrast', 'unlike'.

The risks of this approach are that it can feel repetitive. You will also probably write a lot about the first work and this can overbalance what you say about the second one. Be sure to give each one the same amount of space.

2 Similarities to differences

In this format you identify what's similar and work through each point. You then identify what's different and work through that. The body of your essay has two large sections, which may have one paragraph – or at most a few paragraphs – in each.

3 Point to point

In this structure you define the major points for comparison, and then work through them one at a time, referring to each work as you go.

Vocabulary

Joining your thoughts up and making the essay cohesive is also important.

To compare things, you need to use words and phrases such as *in the same way, similarly, as well as, also, likewise, both*.

To contrast things, you need words and phrases like *although, however, in contrast, on the other hand, instead, on the contrary*.

See page 254 for a more detailed list of transitional words and phrases that can help you here.

{PART 5}

WRITING SUPPORT

1
WORDS THAT WORK

In this section you'll find 'cheat sheets' and lists to help you with different writing formats.

Text type	Audience	Purpose	Context	Content suggestions	Language
Advertisement	Potential customers	Sell something	Newspaper, brochure, online, billboard	Descriptions that make the goods sound attractive, give information about price, where to buy; images	Persuasive, emotional, exciting, appealing; high modality
Diary	Yourself	Remember something that happened	Personal, written in a book	Feelings and reactions as well as descriptions of what happened	First person; intimate register; emotional, candid (open), confidential tone

Words that work

Text type	Audience	Purpose	Context	Content suggestions	Language
Book or film review	Audience the book or film is aimed at	Preview the story and evaluate (say whether it's good or not)	Public (magazine, online)	Plot summary, evaluation of how well it works; background information to enhance appreciation (for example, comments on the actors, setting, art direction and film techniques)	Evaluative, giving opinion with examples, facts and information in the mix; casual or semi-formal register
Information report	Class or teachers	Describe what happened (for example, a science experiment)	School	Factual description of what was done, comment on how it went, overall evaluation	Objective, unemotional, descriptive; formal register
Appliance instructions	Users	Explain procedure	Leaflet, or printed on box or packaging	What to do, sequenced step by step	Simple, clear, plain language; unambiguous
Creative writing	People like you	Entertain, interest, captivate	School, competition	Whatever you like within the guidelines of the question	Must suit the subject
Persuasive writing	Real or imagined – as directed	Change minds and actions	School	Problem, solution, benefits; reasons for change	A mix of emotion, facts, information and reasons
Analytical writing	Teachers, markers	Show you understand a text and can analyse it	School, exams	Strict five (or more) paragraph structure	Builds an argument; thesis, explanation, quotes, analysis

Arranging your arguments

The term **pattern of arrangement** means how you set out your views. It's like arranging the furniture at home. There are many ways to go about it. The question is what will work best and suit the information you are working with. Here are some options.

Arrangement	How it's done	Sample outline
Topical	Divides the topic into different categories of information	Sydney is a great place for families to live. There are three reasons: the economy, the landscape, the recreational opportunities.
Spatial	Creates a 'tour' of a place, idea or object	Central Australia is a good holiday destination. Let's look one-by-one at Uluru, Kata Tjuta and the MacDonnell Ranges.
Cause – effect	Explains how and why something has occurred	The origins of the First World War lay in the alignment of power blocs in late 19th-century Europe (then step it through in an orderly sequence).
Problem – solution	Describes a current problem or harm, and provides a way to overcome it	Drug use, alcohol consumption and street violence have made city streets unsafe. It's costing lives. We need better street lighting, more police on the beat, and late-night public transport to protect people and restore safety to the area.

Words that work

Arrangement	How it's done	Sample outline
Chronological	Good for describing things in sequence as they occurred	Daceyville was created in 1912, as a model 'garden suburb' for the working class. From 1916, returning soldiers moved in. By 1924 there were six shops, a baby health clinic, a large community hall, a police station and one public school. In the 1970s the suburb was to be bulldozed, but resident protests and green bans saved it. It remains protected by a development control plan.
Compare and contrast	Proves the merits of one idea or proposal over another. 'On the one hand ... on the other hand ...'	The character of Shylock is, on the one hand, proud, mean and grasping. On the other hand, we can see that he has suffered a lifetime of insults and ridicule, and his hardness is a way of protecting himself.

And here are some diagrams that you can use to help you plan your work.

Chronological

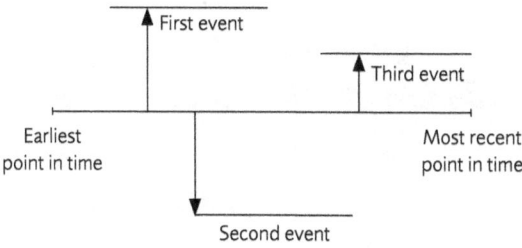

Part 5: Writing support

Compare / Contrast

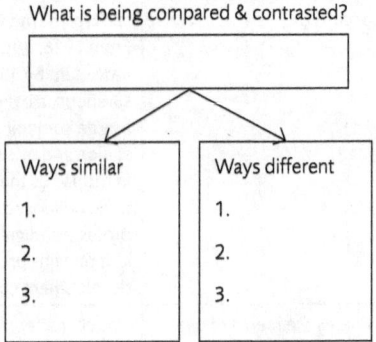

Topical, Spacial or Chronological

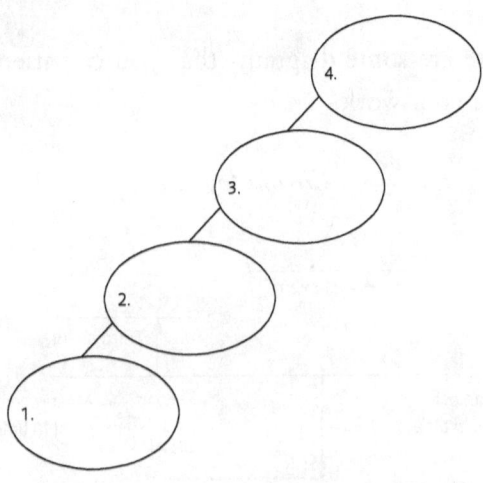

How to persuade with ethos, pathos or logos

	Persuading with ethos	Persuading with pathos	Persuading with logos
Being positive – you are for something	Appeal to values that wear the 'halo of goodness': fairness, truth, patriotism, safety, trust, honour, respect, justice, kindness, family, love, care, responsibility. Use expressions such as 'it's not right to', 'it's unfair that'. Often an expert opinion plays a part.	Stir strong feelings by using emotive (high modality) language, emphatic statements, overstatement, forceful assertions. Address the audience directly: 'have you ever', 'don't you realise that', 'we are all affected by'. Call up feelings like pain, suffering, joy, relief. Include a call to action: 'you can help', 'together we can'.	Keep a calm tone, use objective language, refer to outside authorities (experts, data, statistics or research studies, witnesses). Mention other views: 'some people think that'. State what an opposing view is and deal with it by showing what's wrong with it.
Being negative – you are against something	Appeal to values that we reject: unfairness, discrimination, selfishness, greed, laziness.	Emotional language that insults or belittles opposing views; bias, sarcasm, claiming there's only one true way, excluding other views, referring to unreliable witnesses and sources.	Distort the picture by offering only evidence and arguments that work for you, using false, imaginary data and made-up stories as proof.
Best language techniques	First-person narrator. Personal opinion and value statements: 'it's wrong', 'I believe that', 'in my opinion'. Rhetorical questions, repetition for effect, figurative language; anecdotes and stories to illustrate.	First-person narrator. Direct appeal to audience: 'you must'. Exaggeration (hyperbole), rhetorical questions, conditional words, imperatives, adjectives and adverbs, repetition for effect, high modality, punctuation for emphasis (exclamation marks, bold, underlining). Figurative language, anecdotes and stories to illustrate.	Passive voice, third-person narrator. Anecdotes and stories to illustrate. Low modality and conditional tense. (See page 254 for a list of persuasive phrases to help you sound reasonable.)

Transitional Phrases

And here's a list of persuasive phrases that you can use to transition and link parts of your argument.

Opinions, beliefs	Disagreeing	Giving Reasons
In my opinion	I don't think that	To start with
I believe that	The problem with that point of view is that	When you consider that
Without a doubt	Let's face it, the truth of the matter is	Allowing for the fact that
I honestly feel that		Considering
As far as I'm concerned	But what about	Many people think
It is certain that	I doubt if	That's the reason why
I'm convinced that	I'd prefer	For this reason
If it were up to me	I don't agree	That's why
The way I see it	Obviously this is wrong because	
I'd far rather	Clearly, this doesn't take into account	Another reason it is the case is that
I think	The trouble with that point is	A strong point in favour is
I'd like to	This is evidence of flawed thinking	A further reason
It's easy to see that	In contrast	Consequently
You can see that	On the contrary	At the same time
There can be no doubt that	On the other hand	As indicated earlier
	However	Further to
	Contrary to	In support

2
EDITING

Content

Have you answered all parts of the question?
Does the opening paragraph prepare the reader?
Is there an introduction, a body and a conclusion?
Does each paragraph have a topic sentence?
Is there an example from the text to support the argument from the topic sentence?
Have you explained the link between your arguments and the essay question?
Have you made a general concluding statement?
Have you summarised your answer to the essay question in your conclusion?

Language

Is your written expression appropriate?
Have you used direct and clear language?
Have you kept your audience in mind?

Are your sentences complete and grammatically correct?
Does every sentence follow logically from the one before?
Are your tenses correct?
Have you proofread aloud for errors?
Have you checked your spelling?

Rounding off

Have you re-read your essay (more than once) looking for any mistakes?
Have you gone back over the instructions for the task to ensure you've met the marking criteria?

3
CREATIVE PLOTS: GENRES EXPLAINED

Here's a quick guide to some of the major genres in fiction and non-fiction writing. You can use it to help you classify a work, or to stimulate your own writing.

Fiction

Comedy makes you laugh. There are many ways to do that: punning and word play, creating characters who do dumb things, spoof (sending something up by exaggerating it), satire (showing how absurd something is, in a mean way), romantic comedy (variations on choosing and losing a love match). Comedy uses everyday language, miscommunication and silly misunderstandings for humorous effect.

Fantasy is set in invented worlds or in a legendary, mythic past. There may be superheroes, warriors, witches, wizards and priestesses. It often involves magic, mystical elements and characters or creatures with supernatural powers, such as talking animals or objects. There's a fight between good and evil. Fantasy stories often involve journeys and quests. In some cases, the magical elements intrude into real life. The narrative usually offers lessons about life and dealing with loss, conflict, sacrifice and transformation.

Horror and suspense aims to evoke fear, terror and revulsion. It's often about the supernatural, with the standard features including werewolves, monsters, haunted houses, ghosts, blood, gore, eerie, creepy, shocking events and nightmares to scare you. (In your own writing you've been warned to avoid this sort of thing. It's too easy to wind up with a weak story, unbelievable characters and plotlines full of potholes.)

Action-adventure or **thriller** is a genre that's all about anticipation and suspense. It's often about a quest or mission – escaping, attacking, finding something. It's physical and can be violent. The aim is to keep the audience on edge through a series of chases, near misses and hair-raising adventures. It usually has exotic locations. There are many subgenres involving soldiers, explorers, police, spies, or even ordinary people caught up in something unexpected, such as a hijacking.

Mystery presents a puzzle to be solved. There will be a detective mastermind and a closed circle of suspects who each have a motive that has to be assessed. The clues – hints and suggestions, as well as evidence – are presented in a way that makes them seem unimportant.

Creative plots: genres explained

The reader is put in suspense and is held there until a solution is found.

Historical fiction takes a real setting and real characters from an earlier era, and brings them to life using a fictional story.

Realistic fiction is set at the time that the author is writing. The story is about something that could actually happen in the author's (and audience's) world. Setting, plot and character are all believable.

Romantic fiction has love as its main theme and the driver of its plot. There's usually a happy ending.

Science fiction stories operate outside the real world. They are usually set in an imagined future and involve the wonders (or disasters) of technology.

Dystopian fiction presents a world where social institutions have broken down. The author takes a troubling element of society that readers will recognise (youth violence, surveillance by government, the nuclear threat) and shows its harrowing effects. A popular sub-genre is **apocalyptic fiction**, where a few survivors are left after the world has come to an end due to a catastrophe: nuclear warfare, pandemic, extraterrestrial attack or something similar.

Non-fiction

Creative non-fiction provides factual information in the form of a story. We expect it to be accurate, but written using the literary features we've learned about; things like setting, plot and character. The most common examples are **biography,** a true story of someone's life; **autobiography**, the story of your own life; **memoir**, which selects just part of a life; and **travelogue**, which tells the story of a journey. Often the story puts the life or experience in a wider cultural or historical context, or what was happening in the world at the time. Narrative non-fiction is not made up, but is researched. It often includes organisational and graphic features to support the text, for example a glossary, pronunciation guide, family tree, photographs, illustrations, charts, diagrams and tables.

4
MORE ADVANCED GRAMMAR

1 Helping (auxiliary) verbs

These words can be used as helping verbs when you are making complex tenses:

Be in its different forms: *am, is, are, was, were, being, been.*
Do: *do, does, did.*
Have: *has, have, had, having.*
Conditionals: *can, could, may, might, must, ought to, should, will, would.*

2 Intransitive verbs and complements – no object!

An intransitive verb has no object. On page 54 I gave you a few examples. I'm afraid I wasn't telling the whole story.

Although a verb like *arrive* is always intransitive, we can add a few words around it to provide some extra information. For example, we often say 'I arrived there'. The booby trap is that *arrived* has stopped working as a normal verb and is now operating as a linking verb. (Remember the test? Substitute part of the verb *be*. Because you can say 'I **am** there', that's the proof that in this example *arrived* is a linking verb.)

Linking verbs are in a class of there own. They don't have objects, they are called **complements**. The idea is that a complement completes the description of the subject. In our example, the word *there* is the complement because it finishes the description of the subject *I*.

If you want to name the place you arrived at, you'll need to insert the preposition *at* to make the sentence work: 'I arrived at school'. However, *school* is not the object of the verb, it's the object of the preposition *at*. I can say 'He died of boredom', but boredom is not the object of the verb, it's the object of the preposition *of*. (See page 83 for more on prepositions governing the objective.) The verb *arrive* is, was, and always will be, intransitive.

3 Direct and indirect objects

In the sentence 'He bought his daughter a car', we can see that the object of the verb *bought* is *car*. But we can also see that his daughter is also affected by the car buying, and is therefore in some way a partial object of the verb. This is known as an **indirect object**.

Think of it this way. The main action of the subject *He* is to buy (verb) a car (direct object): 'He bought ... a car'. But he buys it for his daughter, who becomes the indirect object of his actions.

Here's another example:

> He passed me the backpack.

The noun *backpack* is the object of the verb *passed*, and *me* is the indirect object of the same verb.

4 Phrasal verbs

These are two- or three-word verbs, and the last word is often a preposition: *get off, look out, break up, give away, fill up, put off, talk over, break in on, look down on, make sure of.* However they function as one verb.

Sometimes you can separate the parts from each other: 'Get that thing OFF me!', 'Fill it up' or 'Talk it over'. But many can't be separated: *look after, wait on, take after.* These pairs are inseparable and must stay together.

5 Complex verb tenses

While the simple tenses described in Part 1 will nearly always do the job, there are more complex tenses that can give additional detail and depth of meaning. This is one of those cases where you use these tenses without thinking. People learning English as a second language have a much harder time of it.

We're going to look at six of them.

Present perfect

You will recall that *perfect* in the name of a verb tense means 'perfected' or 'finished'. Whatever the action was, it's over. (See pages 41–42 to refresh your memory.)

In the **present perfect** tense, *have* (present tense) is used as the helping verb.

> I *have dropped* it.
>
> I *have swum* in that pool.
>
> I *have walked* there.

The main verb is the **past participle** form (see page 41).

This tense tells us that something happened in the past but you're not saying exactly when. Perhaps the exact date and time are not important. Depending on the rest of the sentence, it might mean the action lasted until something else happened.

> I have walked around this town until my feet ache.

Notice that two tenses are mixed together in one sentence: we use *have* (present) while the verb *walked* is the **past participle**. Cool, huh?

More advanced grammar

Past perfect

We call this the **past perfect** tense because the helping verb *had* is in the past. The main verb is once again the past participle.

> I *had walked* that way home.
>
> I *had swum* before it rained.

You use the past perfect tense to say that something was completed in the past, but earlier than something else, which also took place in the past. A second thing is involved: walking before getting home, swimming before the rain came.

Future perfect

The **future perfect** tense describes an action that will be completed some time in the future. Yes, I know that sounds strange. We are time-travelling forward, and then looking back and describing an action that will be completed later than now. It uses *will have* as the helping verb.

> I *will have* swum twenty laps by ten o'clock.
>
> Next Tuesday I *will have* walked that way for the last time.

Notice that the tenses are mixed up again. *Will have* makes it future, but the main verb is once again a past participle: *swum, walked*.

Continuous

Available in all three time frames – past, present and future – the '-ing' ending of the verb (the **present participle**) is the clue that this is the continuous tense.

> **Past**: 'I *was studying* Shakespeare.' This means the action wasn't completed. Often what comes next is 'when …', and something else happens: 'I was studying Shakespeare when I decided to be an acrobat.'
> **Present**: 'I *am studying* Shakespeare.' The action is going on right now.
> **Future**: 'I *will be studying* Shakespeare.' It's going to take place at some time in the future.

Perfect continuous tenses

These three are blends. They use *have* or *had been* and a present participle '-ing' word.

> **Past**: 'I *had been wanting* that role'. The action started and finished in the past.
> **Present**: 'I *have been trying* to learn the lines'. The action began sometime in the past and is still going on.
> **Future**: 'I *will have been waiting* to hear for a week …'. The action taking place will end some time in the future.

More advanced grammar

Conditional tense

On page 42 we met the **conditional tense**. It's about things that haven't happened, but that might or could happen if certain conditions are met. Remember 'if ... then ...'? That's why we call it 'conditional'.

The words you need for constructing conditional sentences are: *if, even if, even though, unless, as long as, on condition that, unless* and *when*.

Conditionals are an important tool for getting people to change their minds or behaviour, because they allow us to see into a possible future. This makes them important for persuasive writing.

The interesting thing about using conditionals is that the *if* clause is in a different tense from the *then* clause.

Here are the three main types of conditional expressions.

1. The present situation and the future outcome are certain:

    If you *tidy* your room, we *will go* for a bike ride.

    Your room is not tidy, but for sure there's a bike ride if you tidy it.

    The *if* clause is **simple present**, and the *then* clause is **simple future**.

2   A hypothetical situation. Something is possible if certain conditions are met.

>   If you *tidied* your room you *could go* for a bike ride.

As the room is not tidy, the result is imagined, but possible, so long as something happens first. Go and tidy your room!

The *if* clause is a **simple past**, and the *then* clause is a **conditional present**.

3   A situation that is completely unreal and imaginary:

>   If you *had tidied* your room you *could have gone* for a bike ride.

The whole chain of cause and effect (tidy room leading to bike ride) is imaginary. None of it happened or will happen.

The *if* clause is **past perfect**, and the *then* clause is **present perfect**.

ACKNOWLEDGMENTS

I had the idea for this book at a funeral. Aged in his 90s, Professor John Gunn had died. His textbook, *Survey of Language*, was a companion to HSC English for my generation, but his daughter – my oldest friend – had no copy. I found two, one for each of us. Re-reading it took me back, to school and university, where his dry wit and droll appreciation of the absurdities and complexities of English had taught me so much. As grammar was phased out of the school curriculum not long after this, I got to thinking about what students since then have missed. It seemed a bit sad.

My good friends Penny and Georgina have been beyond generous with their time and expertise. Each has been invaluable, with scrupulous reads and re-reads of the manuscript, corrections and acerbic yet humorous suggestions. I can never thank them enough for their help.

My husband Michael was always ready and happy to research, verify and clarify. Our daughter Eleanor, a fine writer herself, was candid in her evaluations, and did a great job of example-collecting.

Acknowledgments

Working with language every day is a pleasure. My thanks to Dr Ian Lambert, Principal of The Scots College in Sydney, for his support; to my colleagues in the English Department; and the students we teach (who are in fact, teaching us).

Finally, my most sincere thanks to Kathy Bail, Elspeth Menzies and all the rest of the team at NewSouth Publishing. For everything.

INDEX

abstract nouns 17–18
action-adventure fiction 258
action words *see* verbs
active voice 55–57
adjectival phrases 25, 131
adjectives 24–32
    atmosphere and imagery 30–31
    Big Red Ball rule (list order) 32
    degree 25–28
    in creating characters 210–11
    non-comparable 27
    precise 29
    writing well with 28–32
adverbial phrases 131
adverbs 75–78
    limiters 75–76
    misplaced modifiers 76–77
    writing well with 77–78
allegory 184–85
alliteration 186
allusion 175–76
analytical writing 232–46
    examples 240
    instructional words in 234–35
    paragraph structure 238–41
    preparing to write 245–47
    retelling the story 241
    step-by-step 233–34
    structural options 242–45
    thesis statements 237–38
'and' 85, 88–89

beginning a sentence with 92
apocalyptic fiction 259
apostrophes 121–24
    after 's' 123
    in place names 124
arguments
    arranging 250–52
    transitional phrases 254
articles (the, a, an) 84
assessment formats 204 *see also* analytical writing; creative writing; marking criteria; persuasive writing
assonance 187
atmosphere 30–31
audience 156–57, 159–60
    tone and 145–46
autobiography 260
auxiliary verbs 40, 261

bias 182–83
biography 260
brackets 117–18
'but' 85
    beginning a sentence with 92

case
    origins of 65
    pronouns and 63–64
central ideas in paragraphs 148
characters 207–8
    changes in 212–13

creating 209–13
describing 210–11
dialogue and 211–12
cheat sheets 248–54
checklists for editing 255–56
chronological arrangement 251–52
clauses 132–34
  clause types 132–33
  unusual clause positions 135–36
  writing well with 133–34
clichés 179–80
co-ordinating conjunctions 85
collective nouns 17
colloquialisms 162–63
colons 116–17
comedy 257
commands (imperatives) 127
commas 112–14
  comma splices 195–96
  in three-item lists 114
common mistakes *see* editing problems
common nouns 16
comparative essays 242
comparable / non-comparable adjectives 27
comparatives 25–28
  irregular 28
compare / contrast arrangement 252
comparisons 77
complements 262
completed actions *see* perfect tenses
complex sentences 129
compound nouns 18, 26
compound sentences 129
conclusions 170–71, 215
conditional tenses 42–43, 268–69
conjunctions 85–92
  beginning a sentence with 92
  cohesion from use of 89–91
  types of 85–86
  writing well with 88–92
'connector' words *see* conjunctions
connotation 172–75
context 156–57, 159–60
continuous tenses 42, 267
contrasts, as rhetorical device 137
conversational language 162–63
correlative conjunctions 86
creative non-fiction 259–60
creative writing 205–20
  characters 209–13
  genres 257–60
  openers 216–17
  planning 206–9
  plot 213–18
  setting 218–20
  writing from life 217

dangling modifiers, editing 197–98
dashes 118–19
declarative sentences 127
definite article 84
degree 25–28
demonstratives 84
dependent clauses 132–33
determiners 84
developing writers, grades for 203
dialogue in creating characters 211–12
dictionaries 101
direct and indirect objects 262–63
direct speech 211–12
doing words *see* verbs
double quotes 120
drafting and writing 168–88
dystopian fiction 259

Index

editing 189–90 *see also* writing support
  checklist 255–56
  content 255
  language 255–56
  rounding off 256
editing problems 191–98
  between – among 194
  could of – would of – should of 191
  dangling modifiers 197–98
  each – every – either – neither 69
  fewer – less 191–92
  it's – its 192
  run-on sentences and comma splices 195–96
  subject–verb agreement 196
  tense trap 194–95
  there – there's – their – theirs – they're 193
  who's – whose 192
  your – you're 194
ellipsis 118–19
English language speakers and learners 6
'-er' form *see* comparatives
'-est' form *see* superlatives
ethos 222–23
  persuading with 253
euphemisms 177–79
exclamation marks 111–12
exclamations 127

fantasy 257–58
fiction genres 257–59
figurative language 172–80
  techniques to use 184–88
figures of speech 179
finite verbs 49, 50
first person narrative voice 72–73

form 159
formal language 146, 164–65
fragments *see* phrases
full stops 111
future perfect tense 265

gender and pronouns 62–63
  'they' as a singular pronoun 69–70
genres 205–6, 257–60
  creative non-fiction 259–60
  fiction 257–59
gerunds 18
grades 201–4
  acceptable answers 202–3
  not quite there yet answers 203
  top answers 201–2
  very good answers 202
grammar, advanced 261–68
  complex verb tenses 263–68
  direct and indirect objects 262–63
  helping verbs 261
  intransitive verbs and complements 261–62
  phrasal verbs 263
grammar basics for great writing 14–92
grammar conventions 7, 14
groups, nouns for *see* collective nouns

helping (auxiliary) verbs 40, 261
historical fiction 259
horror and suspense 258
hyperbole 176
hyphens 119

ideas 171, 206
idiom 176–77
imagery 30–31, 177

imperatives (commands) 127
indefinite articles 84
independent clauses 132
indirect objects 262–63
informal language 162–63
'ing' words *see* continuous tenses; gerunds
instructional words in analytical questions 234–35
interrogative sentences 127
intimate language 162
intransitive verbs 54, 261–62
introductions 169–70, 213–14, 237–38
inverted commas 120–21
irregular comparatives and superlatives 28
irregular verbs 34–36

jargon 180–81
'joining' words *see* conjunctions

language registers 160–65
   what not to do 166–67
language techniques *see* figurative language
limiters (adverbs) 75–76
linking, role of conjuctions in 89–91
linking verbs 44–47
literary techniques *see* figurative language
locator words *see* prepositions
logos 222–23
   persuading with 253
'-ly' endings *see* adverbs

manipulative language 182–83
marking criteria 200
marks, writing for 200–246
memoir 260

metaphor 184–85
misplaced modifiers 76–77
mistakes *see* editing problems
modality 188
modifiers *see* adjectives; adverbs
'more' and 'most' 26–28, 77
multi-subjects 50
multi-word nouns *see* noun phrases
mystery fiction 258–59

names *see* place names; proper nouns
narrative non-fiction 206
narrative voice 74
narrative writing 205–20
nominalisation 20
non-comparable adjectives 27
non-finite verbs 49, 50
noun phrases 20, 130
   in creating characters 210–11
nouns 16–23
   compound 18, 26
   in creating characters 210–11
   precise 21–22
   proper 22–23
   that relate 22
   when and where information from 22
   writing well with 20–23
noun types 16–18
number, pronouns and 62–63

objective case 63–64
   prepositions and 83
   pronouns and 67, 70
objects 50–51, 54
   direct and indirect 262–63
   intransitive verbs and 261–62
omniscient narrators 72–73
onomatopoeia 185

Index

openers, in creative writing 216–17
order of words *see* syntax
organising principles *see* structural options in analytical writing

paragraphs 147–51
    as separate but related parts 149–50
    logical flow 148–49
    PEEL mnemonic 227–29
    persuasive 227–29
    single idea in 148
    structure of 238–41
    variety and balance 150–51
parentheses *see* brackets
parsing 40
participles
    dangling 197–98
    past and present 41
parts of speech 14–15
    part-of-speech confusion 26
    testing 21
passive voice 55–57
past participles 41, 264
past perfect tense 265, 268
pathos 222–23
    persuading with 253
PEEL mnemonic 227–29
perfect tenses 41–42, 263–68
periods *see* full stops
personification 185
'persons' 38–39
    pronouns and 62–63
    third person narrative voice 72–74
persuasive writing 221–31
    ethos, pathos and logos 222–23, 253
    getting the marks 229–31
    persuasive language 224
    planning 225–27
    rhetorical triangle 223–24
    transitional phrases 254
    writing persuasive paragraphs 227–29
phonics *see* sounds
phrasal verbs 263
phrases (fragments) 130–32
    unusual positions 135–36
    writing well with 131–32
place names, apostrophes in 124
planning writing 156–67
    analytical writing 245–47
    audience 156–57, 159–60
    context 156–57, 159–60
    creative writing 206–9
    persuasive writing 225–27
    purpose 156–58
plot 207–8, 213–18
    six steps to a great story 213–15
    1. introductory sections 213–14
    2. complications 214
    3. rising action 214
    4. climax 214
    5. resolution 214–15
    6. conclusion 215
    overcomplicated plots 218
plurals 19
    apostrophes not part of 122–23
    singular / plural confusion 52–53
point of view *see* narrative voice
possession
    apostrophes and 121–24
    possessive case 64
    possessives 84
predicate 48
prefixes 105–6

preparing to write *see* planning writing
prepositional phrases 81, 131
prepositions 79–83
  as a 'closed group' 79
  different meanings of 81–82
  objective case and 83
  pronouns and 70–71
  sentences ending with 83
present participle 41
present perfect tense 264, 268
principal clauses, delaying 134–38
pronouns 58–74
  between you and I, it is I 70–71
  case and 63–64
  each, every, either, neither 69
  he, she, they 69–70
  how they work 62–64
  person, number, gender and 62–63
  problems with 66–71
  replacing yourself + 1 66–67
  what pronouns are 59–61
  what pronouns are not 61
  writing well with 71–73
pronunciation *see* sounds
proofreading 190–98
proper nouns 16–17, 22–23
punctuation 108–24
  change of meaning through use of 109–10
  origins of 110
  punctuation marks 110–23
  reasons for 109–10
  speech and quotes 120–21
  to end sentences 111–12
  to slow down 112–17
  to wait briefly 117–19
purpose, in planning writing 156–58

qualifiers *see* adjectives; adverbs
question marks 111
questions (as sentences) 127
quotation marks 120–21

realistic fiction 259
reflexive pronouns 64
registers *see* language registers
regular verbs 34–35
repetition, as rhetorical device 137
rhetorical devices 137
rhetorical triangle 223–24
rhyme 187
rhythm 186
romantic fiction 259
root words 106
rounding off, in editing 257
rubric 200
rules of English 6–9
run-on sentences 113, 195–96

science fiction 259
semi-formal language 163–64
semicolons 116
sentence diagramming 139
sentences 125–39 *see also* syntax
  beginning with 'and' or 'but' 92
  ending with a preposition 83
  parts of 129–34
  punctuation at end of 111–12
  sentence types 126–29
  variety and balance in 150–51
  verbs in 126–27
  writing better 134–38
settings 207–8, 218–20
  detail in 219–20
'she' 69–70
silent letters 97
simile 184
simple sentences 128

Index

simple tenses 41
   simple future tense 41, 268
   simple past tense 41, 269
   simple present tense 268
single quotes 120
singular / plural confusion 52–53
singular words 19
skills for writing well 3–4, 94–151
slang 162–63
smartphones, spelling and 102–3
sounds
   changes in pronunciation 107–8
   spelling and 95–96
spacial arrangement 252
speech marks 120–21
SPEECH mnemonic 226–27
spelling 94–103
   changes in 102–3
   improving 99–101
   Johnson's Dictionary 101
   learning to spell 95–96
   personal bloopers 103
   personal spelling books 100–101
   sources of confusion 96–98
spelling lists 100–101
statements 127
stimuli for creative writing 206
stories *see* creative writing
structural options in analytical writing 242–45
structure 168
study of English 6–10
   labelling in 9–10
   rules in 6–9
subject–verb agreement 49, 196
subjective case 63–64, 66–67
subjects 48–51
subordinate clauses 132–33
subordinating conjunctions 85–86

suffixes 105–6
superlatives 25–28
suspense fiction 258
sustained metaphor 184–85
syntax 140–44 *see also* sentences
   inversion 143–44
   poor 142

technical skills for writing well 94–151
tenses 39–43
   complex tenses 263–68
   editing of 194–95
   mixing tenses 43
   multiple tenses 43
thesis 234, 237–38
   developing a thesis statement 237–38
'they' as a singular pronoun 69–70
third person narrative voice 72–74
thrillers 259
'to be' 44–47
tone 145–46
topical arrangement 252
transitional phrases 254
transitive verbs 54
travelogues 260
triads, as rhetorical device 137

usage 14

verbs 33–57 *see also* tenses; 'to be'
   advice for use of 57
   in sentences 126–27
   linking verbs 44–47
   what, who and when told by 35–40
vocabulary 104–7
   analytical writing 246
   building 106–7
   learning new words 106–7

voice, active and passive 55–57

who or whom 51
who's or whose 192
word families 104–5
word order *see* syntax
words
   change in function of 26
   making new words 106
   origins of 7–9, 36, 65, 101, 107–8, 183
writer's toolkit 171–88
   figurative language 172–83
   figurative techniques 184–88
   ideas 171
writing better sentences 134–38
   adding rhetorical devices 137
   delaying principal clauses 134–35
   starting each sentence differently 137–38
   using unusual clause and phrase positions 135–36
writing process 154–55 *see also* writing well
   drafting and writing 168–88

how to be a good writer 154–98
   planning 156–67
   revision 154–55
   steps in 154–55
writing support 248–69
   cheat sheets for writing formats 248–54
   creative genres explained 257–60
   editing 255–56
   words that work 248–54
writing well 2–3 *see also* writing process
   persuasive writing 227–29
   technical skills for 94–151
   with adjectives 28–32
   with adverbs 77–78
   with clauses 133–34
   with conjunctions 88–91
   with good spelling 98–103
   with nouns 20–23
   with phrases 131–32
   with pronouns 71–73
   writing for marks 200–246
   www.etymonline.com 102

www.ingramcontent.com/pod-product-compliance
Lightning Source LLC
Chambersburg PA
CBHW021804220426
43662CB00006B/179